Guide to Self:

The Beginner's Guide to Managing
Emotion and Thought

by
John L. Schinnerer, Ph.D.

Bloomington, IN Milton Keynes, UK

authorHOUSE

AuthorHouse™
1663 Liberty Drive, Suite 200
Bloomington, IN 47403
www.authorhouse.com
Phone: 1-800-839-8640

AuthorHouse™ *UK Ltd.*
500 Avebury Boulevard
Central Milton Keynes, MK9 2BE
www.authorhouse.co.uk
Phone: 08001974150

First published by AuthorHouse 8/28/2006

ISBN: 1-4259-5388-3 (e)
ISBN: 1-4259-5387-5 (sc)

Printed in the United States of America
Bloomington, Indiana

This book is printed on acid-free paper.

Acknowledgments

This book is dedicated to
My mother and father who helped educate me
My in-laws who helped support me
My children who continue to be patient with me and teach
me patience and
My wife, Kristin, who taught me how to love and who
supports my dreams.
I am eternally thankful to you all!

Table of Contents

Forward

In his book, *Guide to Self: The Beginner's Guide To Managing Emotion and Thought*, Dr. John Schinnerer shares invaluable insight and tools for building a solid foundation for a happy and fulfilled life. He skillfully leads us along a path where self-discovery is enjoyable, rather than something to be feared. Although many people feel that the process of growth and self-examination is inherently painful, Dr. Schinnerer has a seamless ability to guide without judgement thereby providing a safe environment for introspection.

Dr. Schinnerer has a gift in leading us to value ourselves: our priorities, motivations, and frailties. Once we are able to appreciate where we've been and who we are, he helps steer our thoughts toward where we want to go. The emphasis is on what we *want* in life, not what may have impeded us in the past. It is as if we were looking at our life's table of contents deciding upon which chapter to add next. The next chapter may not be a leap in the right direction, but the first in an endless series of steps. The forward steps far outnumber the occasional, and expected, backward steps. Though we set our sites high, falling still leaves us at a higher level than where we were when we began the journey.

As a result of Dr. Schinnerer's coaching, using the same techniques and principles that are presented in this book, the positive changes in my life are immeasurable. My family, friends, and co-workers have all noticed profound growth in my maturity, empathy, and intrinsic happiness. My children are thriving, as I am able to provide a more joyous, focused, and balanced home-life.

While my personal relationships continue to flourish, for the first time in years I am able to enjoy being alone. This gives me time to savor where I am and confidently monitor my course.

For this, I can only thank Dr. Schinnerer for his gift, skill, and passion for helping others. Thank you, Dr. John!

Amy Smoller

Overview

Throughout the world, there is a movement underfoot. It is a movement of millions of people, each of whom seeks meaning in their life. People are searching for a profound happiness which blends science with spirituality. The very purpose of our life seems to be to move towards happiness.

Yet, in my doctoral program in psychology at U.C. Berkeley, I was taught that the best we could hope for was to help clients move from neurotic suffering to normal surviving. Medicine and psychology have been focused on what's wrong with us for the last 100 years. We have been satisfied with simply shoring up our weaknesses when we need to be striving towards a thriving life of purpose and passion. When mental health workers talk about mental health, wellness or well-being, they are merely speaking of the absence of symptoms, disease or distress. For years, the goal for which we've been told to strive (by the medical community) is simply to be free of negative symptoms (e.g., bone fractures, bodily pain, thought disorders, mood disorders, and anxiety).

Only recently have we started to focus on what is right with us, what our strengths are, and how we can systematically go about developing those strengths in order to build a happy and meaningful life. This book is intended to lay out the steps necessary to help you move from irritable to surviving to thriving; from experiencing predominantly negative emotions to primarily positive ones. In short, this book is designed to help you create a life of profound and purposeful happiness.

The latest studies, up through June, 2006, show that you can go from surviving to thriving.[1] In fact, it is becoming clear that there are six areas of life that must be mastered for a life of true happiness and meaning. Research done in the past six years make a compelling case for the notion that these key areas include an active spiritual life, management of emotions, realistic optimism, lifelong physical fitness, clear values, and supportive relationships.[2,3,4,5,6,7,8]

This book is the first in a series of books which will address all six of these areas for a thriving life. This book focuses on thoughts and emotions – the two areas which serve as the foundation for a truly happy and meaningful life. Happiness is primarily a function of your internal landscape – thoughts and emotions. The first step towards happiness takes place inside you – in your heart and your mind.

Unless stated otherwise, the information in this book is proven by peer-reviewed research, the gold standard of scientific information. I have woven research findings in with my own experiences and numerous counseling sessions to make for an easy read.

"*Guide To Self*" walks the reader through a straightforward approach to mental and emotional well-being, values and healthy relationships. "*Guide To Self*" lays out an approach to living life in a purposeful and peaceful way. This approach has been proven to be highly successful with counseling clients as well as coaching clients on the Guide To Self radio show, including one gentleman who lost every item he owned in Hurricane Katrina. The approach replaces emptiness, exhaustion and depression with purpose, pride and contentment.

> "*Very few people ever really are alive, and those that are never die, no matter if they are gone. No one you love is ever dead.*"
> Ernest Hemingway

This book focuses on the two areas out of the six required for a successful and happy life, the management of thoughts and emotions. Subsequent books will address the other four areas. The six areas necessary for a thriving life are contained in the acronym InSPIRE:

1. **Inward-looking** – happiness is found primarily on the inside; only 20% of happiness is external (e.g., material items, relationships, wealth), the remaining 80% is a result of internal changes in thought, feeling and perception.

2. **Spiritual** - identify top five values so you can behave in accordance with them; believe in and have a personal, daily relationship with your higher power

3. **Physical** - guidelines for physical health, the foundation of all energy
4. **Intellectual** – learn to manage your thoughts
5. **Relational** - identify and handle life leeches; improve boundaries and communication
6. **Emotional** - manage destructive feelings; cultivate positive feelings

As you learn to hone and balance each of these six areas, you will enjoy an increasingly positive outlook, success at home and work, and a purposeful life.

Based on the latest work in psychology, physiology and psychoneuroimmunology, "*Guide To Self*" will show you step-by-step how to manage your thoughts and feelings to realize your potential and bring out your best. In addition, "*Guide To Self*" takes a holistic approach to life, incorporating the physical, spiritual, and relational into the framework as well as the mental and emotional.

The goal of this book is to show you how to become an exceptional human being and inspire you to take charge of your own feelings, thoughts and actions, ultimately resulting in more happiness. The goal is to do all this while being entertaining and humorous.

While seemingly revolutionary, Dr. John's message is clear: *You are far more powerful than you ever dared to dream. You can have a profound impact on your happiness.*

"Guide To Self" will achieve the following goals:

- Provide current best practices for a thriving and meaningful life based on cutting-edge research.

Emotional Arena

- Offer a new model of emotions which explains the purpose of negative and positive emotions.
- Share methods to manage each of the major negative emotions (i.e., fear, anger, and sadness).

One key to a happy life is management of unhealthy, negative emotions.

- Provide concrete exercises to foster positive emotions (i.e., happiness, passion, and excitement) naturally and easily.
- Share a model of forgiveness which can be used to release old, pent-up anger and disappointment.
- Share a key secret of world class athletes: the power of staying in the present moment.

Mental Arena

- Share the top 10 types of Gremlin, or negative, thinking and the best ways to challenge them.
- Show how to replace Gremlin thoughts with realistically optimistic thoughts.

You can retrain your brain at any age. The brain is like a muscle. Use it or lose it.

Introduction

At the age of 27, while working towards my Ph.D. at U.C. Berkeley, I found myself in charge of the psychological needs of a middle school of 600 students. I was testing and diagnosing students as fast as I could. Another part of my job was running counseling groups for troubled students.

At every school I worked, I was given the boys with the worst behavior problems in the school. One middle school group was made up of eight boys each of whom was roughly 12 years old. I saw them once a week and chatted with them about things they liked to talk about. I created a connection with them. We had a rapport.

Middle school is interesting because the social hierarchy is so clearly formed by the age of 11. There is a pecking order. There are the cool kids, the geeks, the outcasts, the skaters and so on. And even within this group of 8 boys, there was a pecking order.

The student at the bottom of the pecking order, let's call him Todd to preserve his anonymity, was the most impulsive of the lot. Todd couldn't stay in his chair, couldn't keep his body still for more than 5 seconds. He had no social skills. He was frequently involved in fistfights with other kids because his mouth would go in motion before his mind caught up. He'd insult a bigger, older student and wind up getting the snot beat out of him every week. The other students teased him mercilessly causing a gradual build up of anger within him.

Now when I run a group, I try to give these students a different response than what they typically get from adults – anger, contempt, and punishment. So I try to be relaxed, calm, and authentic.

One day, I was running the group as usual and the boys were more stirred up than usual. Todd, in particular, was agitated and wound more tightly than normal.

Towards the end of the hour, for some unknown reason, Todd sprung out of his chair, hopped the table and ran towards me. As he closed on me, he made a fist and took a swing at my face. I did not make any attempt to stop him. Todd's fist stopped an inch from my nose. Apparently, he had some self-control after all.

Being a school psychologist was like being a referee at a hockey game - non-stop action. Who knew psychology would involve fisticuffs?

My eyes met his and then looked down at his fist. I had a choice to make. Do I send him to the vice-principal for discipline or do I take a risk and treat him differently than every other adult in his life treated him? Rather than send him to the vice-principal for discipline, I told him he had a choice: take his seat or return to class. He chose to take his seat.

I turned to the group and asked them, "Okay, now what just happened?" The boys were stunned. It took a few minutes to get anyone to say anything. Eventually, one boy said he saw Todd take a swing at me and I did not respond. He said he had never seen anything like it. In his world, anger was *always* met with anger. It was inconceivable to respond any other way, until that moment. And it's true; anger is nearly always met with anger because anger is contagious. You can "catch" anger from someone else...unless you know how to stay calm in the face of anger. Over the next two years, I received calls from nearly every one of those boys' mothers to inquire about private individual counseling. That day had a profound impact on how those boys viewed the world around them. That moment spoke to the emotional part of their minds. And that is a perfect segue into a discussion about the human mind and how best to think of it.

For thousands of years, philosophers, authors and scientists have searched for an adequate metaphor to describe the human mind. In fact, your entire way of thinking is founded on language and metaphor. You are bound by the language you use to describe the world around you. For instance, it's difficult to think about life in the abstract, or even long-term.

However, once the metaphor of life as a journey is applied, the metaphor provides a framework in which you can think about life. The metaphor of life as journey implies that it's a good idea to discover which direction you're headed, who you're going with, and to expect some ups and downs. It is far easier to make sense of complex ideas with the right metaphor – the right language.

Along these lines, humankind has likened the mind to many different wild animals. For instance, Buddha compared the human mind to a wild elephant.

The philosopher, Plato, used an allegory of the human mind as a charioteer holding the reins of two horses where the calm, reasonable part of the mind is the chariot driver, the soul is the chariot, one horse represents the virtues and the other horse is the animal appetites and desires.

More recently, Jon Haidt, professor of psychology at University of Virginia and author of *The Happiness Hypothesis*, compared the mind to a rider atop an elephant where the rider is the rational, conscious mind and the elephant is the emotional, unconscious, automatic part of the mind.[9]

There is a reason that humankind has compared the mind to wild animals for thousands of years – because it's an apt comparison. When I talk of the human mind, my audiences find it easiest to think of the mind as one of two metaphors:

1)   A rider atop a wild stallion or

2)   An alligator hunter wrestling an alligator.

The mind is like a rider atop an elephant.

In both metaphors, the person (the rider or the alligator trainer) represents your conscious, rational side of the mind and the stallion or alligator represent your unconscious, primal, emotional, automatic side of the mind. For the first metaphor, the rider is your thoughts and the wild stallion is your emotional, primal mind. Using the second metaphor, the person training the alligator is like your thoughts and the alligator is like your emotions. Throughout the book, you can use whichever metaphor works best for you. The metaphor you use should be one that resonates with you.

Personally, I'm partial to the alligator and the alligator wrestler which I think is an excellent metaphor for our mind. It's not so much the alligator wrestler part that I like. I love the alligator as an allegory for our emotions. Alligators lay in wait, just beneath the surface of the water, just as intense feelings lie in wait just beneath the surface of our emotional masks. Both alligators and emotions pounce suddenly,

The mind is also like a person wrestling an alligator!

without warning, when their prey comes along. Emotions and alligators are primitive; aggressive throwbacks to an ancient, fierce time. And more, the word, alligator is taken from the Spanish *"el lagarto"* which translates as "the lizard." The emotional part of the brain is considered the limbic system which is also known as the "lizard brain."

Both alligators and emotions, lie just under the surface waiting to pounce.

Alligators are known for their death roll. Alligators drown their prey and rip them apart limb from limb by aggressively rolling over several times, back and forth. Rage and fear are also (emotional) death rolls and threaten to end in violent confrontation with others each time they arise.

Alligators have been shown to be an integral part of the ecosystem, creating holes for other animals to live in and keeping and are considered to be an integral species for maintaining the system's integrity. This relationship holds true for emotions as well which are integral for the proper function of humans.

We need emotions. We cannot simply turn off emotion and live as logical cyborg-like beings. We could not exist solely with our rational mind. We would not know how to make decisions, tag events as dangerous or even which general direction to head in without emotion.

I have spent my entire life exploring the hidden terrain of the mind. I have studied philosophy, quantum physics, psychology, physiology, and world religions. I have spoken with the mentally ill and the psychologically resilient. And this book is my attempt to put forth the latest ways to tame your wrestler and alligator – your thoughts and emotions.

For many years, I was able to suppress my own emotions in stressful situations. I had excellent control over the alligator wrestler but little awareness of how to manage the alligator. Despite my Ph.D. in psychology, I struggled to stay on an even emotional keel day-to-day. I would get irritable with my family. I would have an occasional angry outburst at an unsuspecting coworker. I would be overcome with sadness for days or weeks.

Since then, I have found ways to manage my alligator. I have learned to train my thoughts to be more realistically optimistic. It took me a great deal of time and energy searching to find ways to train my thoughts, and release harmful emotions. I have found tools and attitudes to help me remain calm amidst the emotional hurricanes brought on by my clients, my coworkers and my family.

Even more amazing to me was that, within the past five years, my family became easy to love. This was in stark contrast to the frustration and irritability that my wife and children used to create in me.

So what changed?

I did.

I changed my outlook from pessimistic to realistically optimistic. I improved my physical health. I learned how to get rid of unwanted anger, sadness and fear. I discovered how to relax and enjoy life. I stopped my negative, self-defeating, punitive thoughts and replaced them with optimistic and supportive ones. I reduced my contact with life leeches, the people who constantly suck you dry of energy. I began speaking to God more frequently. I slowed my pace down. And I learned to smile more easily.

Despite *having* everything, I used to be irritable and moody. When I became sad, I would stay down for days or even weeks at a time. When something made me angry, I could not shake the anger. Fear gripped me much of the time. People made me anxious. My muscles were always tense. I never took a deep breath. It was like my emotional gas tank was filled to the brim with negative energy – fear, anger and sadness. It was as if the world had hurt me so badly so frequently that I never got the chance to recover from one traumatic blow before getting hit by the next one. I sometimes wonder if all of us aren't stuck in the grieving process somewhere.

From the perspective of an outsider, everything looked fine in my life. On the inside, I was drowning. I tried everything to escape from my perfect façade of a life – drinking, counseling, overachieving, medication, education – and none of it worked. These did not work because none of them addressed my life as a whole. They were a shotgun approach to a complex problem – the problem of human existence.

Now, things are different. I went from smart to happy. My patience has grown. I find joy in life's little nuances. I live in the present. I am more authentic in the sense that my outer appearance is an accurate reflection of my inner state. I am passionate yet peaceful in my own skin. Most importantly, there are proven ways in which you too can build up your inner reservoir of energy to become more resilient, more balanced, and more content.

My suggestion to you is to approach this book and, most importantly, life from the perspective of a student for whom learning is a never-ending quest; approach life as a novice with an attitude of awe and reverence. Search for meaning in every event and every action. Lifelong learning and meaning-making are two critical aspects to resiliency and will begin your journey towards contentment and meaning.

Recently, Barbara Fredrickson, a professor of psychology at University of North Carolina, made the discovery that *it takes three times as much positive emotion as negative emotion to lead a thriving life.*[10] My intention in writing this book is to help you reduce the frequency and intensity of negative emotions and increase the frequency and intensity of positive emotions you experience. My goal is to point you in the right direction; a direction where you can make your own choices from an authentic place. When you begin making choices from an authentic place -- a blend of heart, mind, spirit and body -- you will inevitably make the right choices. And, in this way, you can heal yourself one choice at a time. And, in time, the world becomes a better place to live, one person at a time.

**Psychological Hotline
1-800-FRUITCAKE**

Hello! Thank you for calling the brand new Psychline!
If you are obsessive-compulsive, please press 1 repeatedly.
If you are co-dependent, please have someone press 2 for you.
If you have multiple personalities, please press 3, 4, 5, and 6.
If you are paranoid, we know who you are and what you want. Just
    stay on the line so we can trace the call.
If you are schizophrenic, listen carefully and a little voice will tell you
    which number to press.
If you are depressed, it doesn't really matter which number you
    press. No one will answer.

The goal of this book is to provide you with some comfort and inspiration. There is a certain world view expressed in the pages of this book. This world view allows for an infinite number of possibilities. And within this myriad of possibilities lies the inevitability of discovering meaning for your life and those around you. This may mean learning assertiveness, overcoming fear or anger, releasing sadness, breathing deeply, praying, tuning in to your body, or finding forgiveness. The goal is to fan the flames of hope and inspiration within you so that you can pursue peace and move on. And, in moving on, share your new found peace with others.

Obsessions

A psychologist was conducting group therapy with four young mothers. "You are all obsessed!" he observed.

To the first mother he said, "You are obsessed with eating. You went so far as to name your daughter Candy."

He turned to the second mom. "Your obsession is shopping. Again, it is seen in your child's name, Penny."

He turned to the third mom. "Your obsession is drinking and your child's name is Brandy."

At this point, the fourth mother got up, took her little boy by the hand and whispered, "Come with me, Dick, we're going home!"

While you are reading, please honor your own sense of playfulness and humor. It is with grave seriousness that I remind you to laugh loud and often. Life makes fools of us all. Those that are best equipped to deal with life cultivate a keen sense of humor which includes the ability to laugh at one's self. Laughter and a sense of perspective offer us a path through trying times. Laughter is the best antidote to suffering. The more you are able to nurture a sense of happiness and an appreciation for life, the more you build up your inner resources which keep you balanced in times of pain.

The question is; how do you build up your inner resources so that you are filled to the top with positive energy, love and compassion so you can perform at your best?

The Overflowing
Emotional Reservoir

Within you there is a reservoir of energy; of emotion.[11] Most people have an overflowing reservoir. The problem is that their reservoirs are overflowing with anger, sadness and fear. To lead a thriving life, it is critical that you discover how to let go of the negative emotions in your reservoir.

An overflowing reservoir of positive emotion is created, in part, by having an accepting and patient outlook. More patience buys you more time to listen to your internal wisdom, the quiet voice in the back of your head that speaks in fleeting whispers. You can cultivate this attitude by asking yourself the question, "Will this matter a year from now?" Most of the times, the answer is "No, it won't matter." It's one of the ways you can learn to be less emotionally reactive and more thoughtfully proactive. You have to train yourself to behave in healthy ways because, if you are like most of us, you did not learn these mannerisms growing up. So you need to *retrain your brain.* As you learn to respond more effectively to minor inconveniences, it leaves you more positive energy to respond to actual crises. This is known to many as wisdom - the ability to deal well with your own suffering as well as help others with theirs.

Imagine if your bucket were filled with positive emotions!

Not only will you learn how to deal more efficiently with your pain, you will also learn how to appreciate life. Life is a gift that has been granted to us. The more you appreciate and cherish the gift, the more you understand what a magical journey life is.

1

The Emotional Mind - Harnessing the Power of Emotions

Emotions are the primary, driving force behind what you say, what you do, what you don't do, what you think and how you perceive the world around you. Think back to the rider astride a wild stallion as a metaphor for the human mind (or alligator and trainer). The person represents your conscious, rational side of the mind; the "you" that you consider "you." The stallion (or alligator) represents the unconscious, emotional, automatic side of your mind.

The scariest journey you can make is into your own emotional land-scape to allay the alligator, to harness the horse, to still the stallion. Feelings scare more people than heights, public speaking and death combined. Part of the reason that emotions are so scary is that a large part of our emotions are outside of our conscious control. *Emotions are largely automatic.* Perhaps because of the fear related to emotions, exploring your emotional landscape is one of the most rewarding activities in which you can engage. As an added bonus, learning more about your emotions and how to manage them will lead to greater success at work, home and in your relationships.

The difficulty in building emotional intelligence lies in the fact that many of your emotional responses are automatic. Your brain automatically appraises situations and people to keep us safe. Your brain is constantly on the lookout for danger. To do this, the brain sidesteps your conscious mind and makes emotional evaluations every second of every day. If your brain is constantly making automatic appraisals, the question becomes, "How automatic are you?" Just how much free will do you truly have? To what degree do you consciously and intentionally choose and control your experiences, thoughts and feelings? To what extent are your emotions, thoughts and actions determined by other things such as outside events such as traffic or relationships or by unconscious drives such as the appetite for power, sex or achievement?

I firmly believe that *emotions are at the root of many of your difficulties in life.* Anger hijacks you and you blurt out hurtful accusations to loved ones. Sadness washes over you and you withdraw from loved ones. Fear overtakes you and you resign yourself to a life without risk. If you want a

---

*Emotions are the **root** of many of the problems in your life. To create a happier life, you must first learn to deal with your feelings.*

happy life, you must begin by developing emotional management skills. It is imperative.

The philosopher Ludwig Wittgenstein wrote, "Nothing is so difficult as *not* deceiving oneself." You deceive yourself everyday of your life. You believe "you" are in control. You're not in control. At least, you don't have as much control as you think you do. You're on auto pilot roughly *90% of the time.* The unconscious, emotional part of your mind has far-reaching influence on your actions.

The extent of this phenomenon hit me recently as I watched my newborn daughter develop her motor skills. My daughter, Molly, is presently learning how to move her fingers and arms to grab objects. She has to consciously think to close her fingers to grasp an item. Yet, in a few weeks, she will have mastered this skill of opening and closing her hand. The skill will have become automatic. She won't have to waste mental energy to grab something. She'll just do it- automatically. And

How automatic are you? Up to 90% of your actions are automatic!

it struck me that human beings are progressions of automaticity. Humans strive to learn a new skill or concept. Once that skill is mastered, it becomes largely automatic (depending on the degree of complexity of the skill).

Here is a simple exercise which will demonstrate the degree to which you are on auto pilot.

When you try this exercise you'll quickly realize that there is much more going on in your body and brain than you are normally aware. There are intrusive thoughts, bodily sensations, muscle twitches, memories, and more.

Emotions are one of the areas of which we are normally unaware unless it is a highly charged feeling such as rage. One of the goals of this book is to make you more aware of your feelings. Another goal is to help you learn

---

Find a watch or clock with a second hand on it. Write down the time at which you begin. Resolve that for the next five minutes you will pay full and constant attention to the movement of the second hand while at the same time being fully aware of your breathing. And think of nothing else. For five minutes. Go ahead. Try it now before you read any further.

to manage your feelings so they are helping you reach your goals, instead of derailing you.

Most of what occurs in our interior emotional landscape is automatic. Negative emotions, sadness, anger and fear, in particular are automatic. Negative emotions don't need a reason to show up. They come unannounced, triggered by memories, similarities between present situation and your past, exhaustion or other things. It's hard to imagine the degree to which our emotions are automatic.

To demonstrate, I want you to imagine the following scenario:

You are walking alone in a dangerous section of town at three in the morning. There are no street lights. The only light comes from a pale moon. Suddenly, you see three large men wearing hooded sweatshirts walking towards you. You become fearful and this feeling of fear releases your adrenaline, making your heart pound, your eyes dilate, your muscles tense, and you run away.

Or perhaps emotion works like this...You notice three men walking towards you. Recognizing the potential for danger, your emotional brain signals your adrenal glands to release adrenaline, making your heart pound, your eyes dilate, your muscles tense, and you are forced to run away. *Then* you feel fear.

It's an old debate: which comes first, the feeling of fear or the bodily reactions we associate with fear (e.g. sweaty palms, racing heart)? Does the fear make you run or is the fear an (automatic) interpretation you use to explain your behavior after the fact?

The latest research has found that it is the latter – that your feelings are in many cases an attempt by your brain to make sense of your actions. They are the label you stick on your behavior that just took place.

And most times, you are not even consciously aware of the cause of your feelings.

What we're finding is that up *to 90% of our behavior is automatic.*

While most of us have a strong desire to believe in some degree of free will and self-determination, it's hard to refute the fact that most of the tasks in our daily lives are driven by automatic, unconscious mental processes. Think of driving a car on the freeway while talking on a cell phone. Your brain is making thousands of interpretations, decisions, and bodily movements of which you aren't even remotely aware as your conscious awareness is focused on the phone conversation. You are simultaneously maintaining pressure on the gas pedal, moving your foot to the break when necessary, monitoring your speed and the speed of other cars around you, judging

Talking on the cell phone while driving maxes out your brain's capabilities and leads to more car accidents.

the temperature inside the car, assessing weather conditions, gripping the steering wheel, adjusting the steering wheel to keep the car in the lane, figuring your best route, taking into account the driving patterns of other drivers around you, scanning for debris in the road, looking for your exit, holding the cell phone and more. And that's just the voluntary movements! That doesn't take into account the involuntary movements such as heart rate, respiration, digestion, and more. All of these things take place while "you" are talking to your friend on the cell phone. The only things in this scenario that are not automatic are the ones that have to do directly with your phone conversation. Everything else, it can be argued, is automatic, routine, and habitual. And this is the primary reason why there are so many car accidents due to cell phone use. The brain is an amazing organ capable of simultaneously processing multiple tasks, but it has limits. It's my belief that we reach those limits when we drive and talk on the phone at the same time, particularly if the phone conversation becomes emotional.

The Rider on a Wild Stallion

One of my favorite metaphors for the human mind is a rider atop a wild stallion where the rider is your conscious, rational, controlled part of the mind and the wild stallion is the irrational, unconscious, emotional part of your mind. Along these lines, there are always two processing systems working within the mind at all times – controlled processes and automatic processes.

Let me explain by way of illustration. Imagine you volunteered for the following experiment. You are given some word problems to solve by a researcher who tells you to come get her when you've finished them. The word problems are surprisingly simple, just unscramble five sets of words and make sentences using four of them. For example, "her see bother usually they" would become either "they usually see her" or "they usually bother her."

A few minutes later, you finish the task and walk down the hallway to find the researcher. You find her but she's talking with someone and isn't aware of you. What do you do?

Well, if half the sentences you unscrambled contained words having to do with rude behavior, such as "rash", "aggressive", "bother", and "intrude", you are far more likely to interrupt the researcher within 120 seconds and say, "Okay, I'm all done. What's next?"

On the other hand, if you unscrambled sentences in which the rude words were swapped with polite words such as "respect", "nice", "courteous", the odds are that you will just sit there passively until the researcher finishes her talk. And you'll wait for up to ten minutes!

The wild stallion is the emotional, unconscious, automatic part of your mind. The rider is the conscious, rational part of your mind.

In another experiment regarding the power of these outside cues over our behavior, a group of people were given a list of words to read, some of the words had to do with stereotypes of elderly people, such as "retirement", "Florida", and "bald". Another group was handed a list of words with no relationship to elderly stereotypes. Sure enough, participants who were "primed" with elderly-related words instantly began acting more in line with the elderly stereotype. For example, they walked more slowly down the hallway and their short-term memory became worse than the control group. So merely reading the list with words related to old age led to forgetfulness. The truly frightening thing about this experiment is that the group given the words related to elderly stereotypes *could not remember any words* about the elderly in the original list of words! So they were influenced by the words and then forgot all about what it was that influenced them.

Here's a fun exercise you can do at home with your family and friends. I will spell out a word and I want you say the word after I spell it out. S... H... O... P. Now say the word I spelled out loud. Now, what do you do when you come to a green light?

It's difficult to come up with the correct answer to the question. Our brain wants to automatically blurt out "STOP!" This is automaticity at work. And its part of the reason why we do things like say stupid and hurtful things when we get enraged; things which we later regret but, once spoken, cannot be taken back. One of the most important tasks in your life is training your horse, the emotional part of your mind, to cooperate with the rider, the rational part of your mind.

Emotions are Largely Automatic

With practice, you'll be able to manage your horse like an expert.

Without practice and awareness, your emotions are largely automatic. This automaticity is one of the main reasons that emotions are so difficult to manage. Your emotions are so engrained in your brain and your behaviors that you hardly realize you have some power over them. Humankind has long thought of emotions as an uncontrollable aspect of our lives. You may not even realize that you have a choice over how you manage your emotions.

Emotional mastery is not easy. It takes some work. Yet it is one of the greatest goals that you can strive for in your lifetime. The rewards for attaining a greater degree of emotional management are vast: greater happiness, reduced risk of heart disease, better immune system functioning, longer lifespan, more satisfaction with life, improved performance at work and home, less risk of depression, more patience, and a higher quality of relationships. The stakes are high. Your very happiness, perhaps your very life, depends on you learning to manage your emotions.

The goal of this book is to help you reach your potential, to become a whole and complete person, to bring out your best. A complete person has the ability to manage their emotions. A complete person has a rich spiritual life. He has control over his thoughts, and acts in keeping with his values. And finally he has healthy relationships. When you have no control over your emotions, they are in control of you. When you don't manage your thoughts, they manage you. When you lack awareness and mastery in any of these areas, you are at their mercy.

The Samurai and Emotional Awareness

There is an ancient Japanese tale that tells of an aggressive, confrontational samurai who commanded a Zen master to explain the concept of Heaven and Hell to him. The Zen master replied with disdain, "You are no more than a cockroach. I will not waste my time with trash like you." The samurai was enraged and drew his sword from its scabbard. He roared, "I will kill you for your disrespect!"

In the face of the Samurai's rage, a peaceful manner came to the Zen master. "That," the Zen master calmly stated, "is hell."

"I will KILL you for your disrespect!"

"Snatch the pebble from my hand, Grasshopper."

Shocked at seeing the truth in what the master observed about the rage that had the samurai in its grip, he regained his composure and put away his sword. The samurai bowed deeply and gratefully thanked the Zen master for his newfound awareness.

"And that," said the master, "is Heaven."

The moral of the story is if you want to change, change your awareness of your self.

Being Emotional vs. Being Emotionally Aware

The sudden "aha" of the samurai to his own vengeful emotions demonstrates the critical difference between being overtaken by an emotion and being *aware* of being overtaken by an emotion. The difference is subtle yet critical.

As the philosopher, Socrates, told us thousands of years ago, "Know thyself." One of the keys to knowing yourself is to be aware of how you feel.

Emotional Hijacking

One of the keys to knowing yourself is to know when you are being hijacked by your emotions. An emotional hijacking is an emotional explosion in which the limbic area of the brain (the emotional headquarters) declares an emergency and overtakes the rest of the brain to attend to

Watch out for emotional hijackings - when the big dog BARKS!

its needs. This takes place rapidly before the neocortex (the intellectual headquarters) has a chance to figure out what is actually taking place, let alone weigh the consequences of the actions. These emotional hijackings are all too common in individuals today. Think back to the last time you "lost it" and blew up at someone – your child, spouse, subordinate, boss, neighbor, the driver of another car. Next time you sense yourself "losing it" remind yourself to breathe deeply and slowly. See if you can take control of your emotions before they take control of you.

Why Learn to Manage Your Emotions?

Learning emotional management is critical because if you're not managing your emotions, they are managing you. And odds are you won't like their management style!

Take sadness for example. Some of the negative effects of sadness on your body include suppressed immune system functioning, clogging of arteries, loss of energy, muddled thinking, poor decision-making, and digestion problems.

How about anger and irritability? A consistent finding in those who have low self-esteem, migraines, ulcers, heart attacks, substance abuse problems, troubled work and interpersonal relationships and frequent job loss is that they are unable to manage their anger.

Or maybe you tend to be the nervous type. People who are overly fearful or anxious have been found to be more irritable, have fewer relationships, worry too much, have muscle spasms, sleep problems, and more stomachaches and headaches.

What is Emotional Mastery?

Emotional mastery is comprised of two main skills, both of which can be learned – emotional awareness and emotional management.

Emotional mastery builds upon the ability to be aware of your emotions *as they take place*, in the present moment. You must learn to recognize the emotion within seconds of its onset. I cannot overstate the importance of this skill. If you are not aware of your emotions, you have no options. Without awareness, you cannot exercise emotional management.

Once you are aware of *how* you feel, then you can choose what to do about it. First, you recognize your feeling, then you have a choice as to how to deal with the feeling.

The second skill is managing the emotion to allow you to have some conscious choice over your actions. Once you can recognize your emotions as they occur, the next step is to learn to deal with them in an appropriate way. One of the most critical skills we are supposed to learn in childhood is the ability to soothe ourselves when we are upset. This means calming ourselves when we are irritated, angry, scared, anxious, sad, or depressed. Most people have failed to learn this skill. It's not a skill that was typically taught in most families because we didn't know any better. Now, we know better.

People who fail to learn emotional management are forever fighting off chronic anxiety, sadness or irritability. Those who learn to manage their emotions persevere to overcome life's setbacks. They are resilient and rebound from disappointments more quickly. They have a positive, optimistic outlook on life.

I will share a number of tools with you throughout this book that will enable you to become aware of your emotions and manage them. The impact on your life will be profound and far-reaching.

The Goals for Emotional Mastery

To simplify things, imagine, as in Figure 1, that you have four parts to your mind: positive thoughts, negative thoughts, positive emotions and negative emotions. When you look at yourself in this manner, you will realize that one of the main goals of emotional management is to minimize the amount of time you spend wallowing in negative emotions such as anger and irritation. You also want to minimize the amount of time spent ruminating about sad or irritating thoughts. On the other hand, you want to maximize the amount of time you spend thinking positive, optimistic thoughts because that has been shown to result in positive emotions.

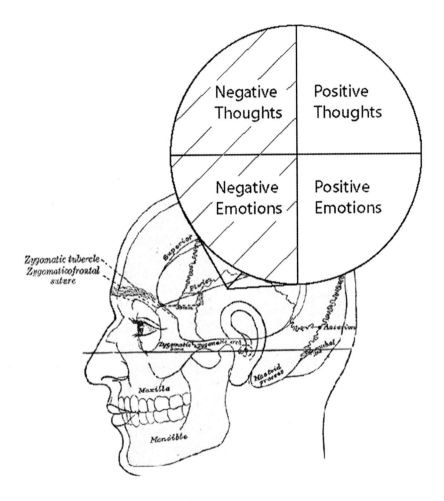

Figure 1. One Way to Divide the Mind

In order to do minimize your negative thoughts and affect and maximize your positive thoughts, and ultimately spend more time bathing in positive emotions, your goals are three-fold.

First, learn to *recognize your emotions in the moment*, honor the emotion, and to release it. This is particularly true for negative emotions.

Second, learn to deal with your emotions in an appropriate manner by *becoming aware* of your current temperament, moods and emotional triggers.

Along the way, I'll also discuss your biologically-determined happiness set point which is the genetically-determined point at which your level

> All of us have slightly different emotional land-
> scapes. We differ in our emotions in terms of:
> How quickly our emotions arise
> How intense they are
> How long they stick around and
> How we share our emotions with others.

of happiness rests. Your happiness set point is the level of happiness or satisfaction that you feel with your life over a long period of time. While your happiness set point is largely determined by your genes, it is possible to change it, to increase your set point so that you enjoy life to a greater degree than before. Thus, the third and final goal of emotional mastery is to *increase your happiness set point so that you are realistically optimistic and your mood is largely content and peaceful.* I'll discuss how to do these things later on in this book.

To start things off, you'll need a deeper understanding of what emotion is and how emotion works.

What is Emotion?

You need to know what emotion is before you can attempt to manage it. So I will discuss the nature of emotion to begin.

Emotion is a difficult term to pinpoint due to the subjective and personal nature of feelings. Despite the fact that emotions vary from person to person in terms of how hard they hit, how quickly they hit, and how long they persist, there are common emotional themes between people that may be brought to light to help you understand these irrational emotions and moods.

Emotion consists of far more than mere moment-to-moment feelings.

> I have had more trouble with myself than with any other man I've met.
> Dwight Moody

Emotion is actually four layers of affective phenomena which include feelings, moods, temperament and the emotional masks you wear to conceal your true feelings.

Psychological energy is comprised of two main components – affective energy (i.e., feelings) and mental energy (i.e., thoughts). I use the words "affect" and "affective" to describe all aspects of feeling which include emotions, moods, temperament as well as the emotional masks you wear.

At the time of the writing of this book, there is still no scientific consensus as to whether thoughts can exist apart from emotion. Most of the time, thoughts are inextricably intertwined with affect. In an attempt to keep things simple and clear, however, I will treat thoughts and emotions separately inasmuch as it is possible.

Affect, or emotional energy, includes four main areas -- emotions, moods, temperament and emotional masks. I will discuss the first three areas together and then discuss emotional masks.

Layers of Affect

Emotions

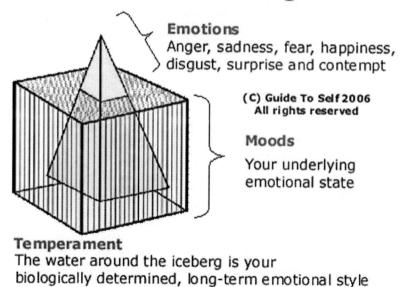

Your Emotional Landscape As The "Iceberg"

Emotions
Anger, sadness, fear, happiness, disgust, surprise and contempt

Moods
Your underlying emotional state

Temperament
The water around the iceberg is your biologically determined, long-term emotional style

Figure 2. Emotions, Moods and Temperament

One way to think of emotion and mood is like an iceberg as in Figure 2. An iceberg is only partly visible from the surface of the water. The bulk of the iceberg lies below the surface of the freezing water. Your emotions are like the 10% above the water that you can see. Your mood is like the

90% below water that is out of sight, below the waterline. Your temperament is like the water in which the iceberg floats. It may be cold (negative), lukewarm (neutral), or warm (positive).

Emotions may also be understood as action scripts, or tendencies, that unfold within a matter of seconds. Normally, an emotion starts with your interpretation of the personal meaning of some event. Sometimes you are aware of this interpretation process and sometimes you are not. In either case, the interpretation causes a cascade of actions that occur across many systems within the body. These actions include changes such as your subjective experience (the feeling inside "you"), your facial expression, your thoughts, and any bodily changes.[12]

The Example of Anger, Irritability and Pessimism

One example of emotion is anger. An old client of mine, Jack, destroyed a friendship of thirty years in a matter of seconds when he was emotionally hijacked by anger. To begin, Jack was in an irritable mood so he was predisposed to becoming angry easily. To add to his irritable mood, Jack was tired and stressed. He also was predisposed to being pessimistic. He had a bad back which pained him greatly. All of these things make it more and more difficult to manage your emotions. Physical pain, stress, a pessimistic outlook, physical exhaustion, and negative moods all have a cumulative, negative effect on your emotions. Each of these make it much more likely you will experience negative emotions such as anger.

After work, Jack met his friend, George, for a drink and a game of pool. One drink led to two drinks and soon enough the pair had downed four drinks. Jack's emotional management ability was nearly non-existent by this time. Along with stress, exhaustion, and negative moods, alcohol and drug use make emotional management highly difficult.

Anger is the short-term emotion.
Irritability is the longer-term mood.
Pessimism is the long-term temperament.

As the night wore on, the two men became more competitive playing pool. Both men were trading insults veiled as teasing. The insults escalated until George made a tasteless, offensive remark about Jack's wife. The attack on his wife sparked Jack's anger. Since Jack was already in an irritable mood, he was predisposed to anger. The anger hit him hard, fast and was difficult to shake.

The emotional, automatic side of his mind (remember the alligator metaphor?) took over control and Jack let fly 15 years of buried anger and resentment. Jack screamed at his old friend about broken promises, debts left unpaid and past betrayals. While the words he spoke to his friend were true, the uncontrollable rage shown by Jack to his friend damaged their relationship forever. Jack's anger-induced words and actions could not be undone. This was a noticeable pattern in how Jack dealt with most people in his life. He buried more and more anger until it burst forth at the wrong time, to the wrong degree and, often, at the wrong person. He frequently screamed at his wife and children. He usually spoke to everyone "beneath" him with a harsh edge of disgust and contempt in his voice. It seemed as though Jack thought that everyone around him was incompetent, lazy or mean-spirited.

After the run-in with George, Jack realized that he was having difficulty dealing with anger and he sought out my help.

I worked with Jack for three months. After three months, Jack told me that found it "hard to be pissed off at anyone anymore." He doesn't get angry nearly as often or as intensely as he once did.

Mood

Underlying and fueling your emotions is your mood. Perhaps the best way to think of a *mood* is as a mild and continuous emotional state. Your mood is your underlying emotional state. You may not even be consciously aware of your underlying mood. Most people are very good at hiding their mood from others and even from themselves. You typically do not share your mood with others, often because you cannot put the right words on it.

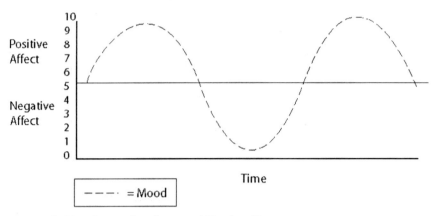

Figure 3. Mood as a Continuous Affective State

For example, an irritable mood (see the filled in section the mood cycle in Figure 4) is most likely to spark feelings of anger at your self, anger at others and disappointment. A depressed mood is most likely to lead to frequent and severe feelings of sadness, remorse, and melancholy. An anxious mood is fuel for feelings of fear and doubt.

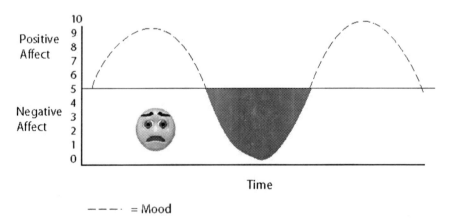

Figure 4. The Negative Mood

A contented mood (see Figure 5) lends itself to more frequent and more intense feelings of joy, happiness and relaxation.

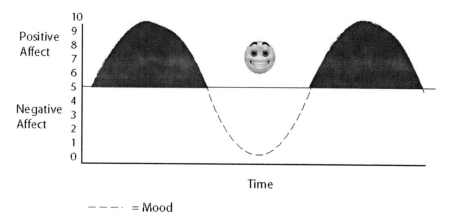

= Mood

Figure 5. The Positive Mood

Your mood predisposes you to feel particular emotions. So if you are in a contented mood, then you are more likely to feel happy, relaxed, and content and less likely to feel angry, sad or fearful (as seen in Figure 6). For instance, when you are in an upbeat mood, nothing gets you down. Minor inconveniences and delays are taken in stride when you're in a good mood. However, when you're in a foul mood, everything sets you off. Little mistakes seem big. Tiny problems appear insurmountable.

The trick is to learn to elevate your mood evenly and consistently while minimizing the amount of time you spend in a negative mood. You don't want to push your mood too high up because what goes up must come down. So if you're mood goes too high, you risk crashing down to earth at some point in the future. Also, if you're mood goes too high, you may be experiencing mania, the 'up' part of bipolar disorder, which is marked by sexual indiscretions, large scale shopping sprees, feelings of invulnerability, lack of sleep and an overwhelming stream of ideas and thoughts racing through your head.

And you don't want to spend too much time in a negative mood because it influences how you perceive the world, increases the degree and frequency of negative emotions and is generally unpleasant for your self and those around you. Remember, the goal is 3 times as much positive emotion as negative emotion for a thriving life. One way to do this is to learn to be aware of and encourage more positive moods which in turn create a greater opportunity for more positive emotions.

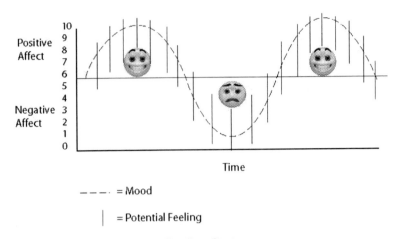

Time

－－－． = Mood

| = Potential Feeling

Figure 6. Mood with Potential Feeling States

Moods can be caused by thought or emotion. Moods are similar emotions strung together over time. Moods can be created by frequent and intense emotional experiences. For example, watching a good comedy makes you laugh, smile, and feel happy. In this way, you can create a good mood.

Another way in which moods can be influenced is via your thoughts. You can think your way to a good mood. If you continually think about love and peacefulness, the consequence will be the emotion of contentment. As you continue to dwell on such positive thoughts, you can move from a singular emotion (happiness) to a continuous positive mood. Keep in mind the golden ratio of 3:1; three parts happiness to every one part sadness or anger or fear. Figure 7 illustrates what an ideal mood might look like for some individuals. It shows more time spent in a positive mood with the occasional dip into a negative mood. Such a mood will aide in achieving the 3:1 ratio.

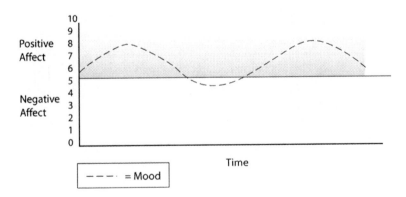

Figure 7. The Ideal Mood for a Thriving Life

One of the main discoveries of positive psychology is that you can consciously generate positive moods by stringing together a series of positive *thoughts*. Use the mental scrapbook approach to recall a series of vacations, funny moments and movie scenes to string a smorgasbord of smiles together.

The ultimate goal is to go through your day thinking kind, compassionate thoughts each and every moment. In this manner, you create new neural networks in your brain that *expect* to feel positively most of the time. So if you find yourself at the bottom of your mood cycle, actively work towards boosting your mood from negative to positive using a series of brief, positive emotions or by thinking of positive things.

Most of us are unaware of our moods and their impact on our behaviors and perceptions. So your moods typically precede and color your thoughts. Most often, this emotional biasing of your thoughts takes place without your conscious awareness – which can frequently lead to negative consequences.

Temperament

The subtlest and broadest layer of affect is *temperament,* the biologically determined set point for your moods and emotions. Temperament is your long-term, emotional style. It is extremely subtle and you may not even be aware of it. Temperament is played out over the span of your lifetime. Most people are born and die with the exact same temperament because they don't realize that they have the power to change it to their liking.

Temperament is the emotional backdrop upon which your emotions and moods are painted. Your temperament is a broad-brush, crude coloring of every thought and perception you have. It is not attached to a specific object or person. You may not even be aware of it. Temperament is the lens through which you see the world. It is most often thought of as a "glass half-full" or a "glass half-empty" outlook.

However, it's my belief that temperament can be one of three valences – positive, negative or neutral. Your glass may be half-full (an optimistic, positive interpretation), half-empty (a pessimistic, negative interpretation) or simply filled with water (a neutral interpretation).

Just as the particles of an atom have three different types of charges, positive, negative and neutral, so too does temperament. The atom has electrons (negative charge), protons (positive charge) and neutrons (neutral charge). Just as electricity has a positive line, a negative line and a neutral ground, so too does temperament.

This means that there are three basic categories of mood and emotion that fit into these three categories of temperament – positive, negative or neutral. Examples of positive emotions include gratitude, joy, love, interest, contentment and mindfulness. The major negative emotions include sadness, anger and fear. The only neutral emotions that have been identified are surprise and confusion.

Differences between Emotions, Mood and Temperament

There are three main differences between the three areas of emotions, moods and temperament -- how long they last, how diffuse they are, and their root causes.

Time

The first difference is temporal – how quickly the affect comes on and how long it lasts. Emotions are measured in milliseconds or minutes. Emotions come over you within a split second (as in Figure 8). Fear takes hold of you within a third of second. The feeling of fear can pass after ten minutes or several hours.

Emotions take place over a much shorter time than moods. Moods are measured in terms of days or weeks.

Seconds	Days	Years

Emotion	Mood	Temperament

Figure 8. Time and Affect

Anxiety is fear spread out over time. Anxiety can last for several days, several weeks or several months. Anxiety is a chronic state of worry which may last anywhere from days to weeks. Anxiety predisposes you to feel fear and apprehension. When you are anxious, you already have begun to move in the direction of fear. You interpret the world around you in terms of perceived threats and dangers when you are chronically anxious.

Irritability is an excellent example of a mood where you are slightly annoyed all the time. When you are irritable, you are always prone to anger. You are predisposed to anger when you are irritable. Neutral situations are interpreted as negative when you are in an irritable mood. When you are irritated, negative situations are viewed as having more negative weight than they may actually have.

Another example of a mood is when you get in a funk, or a mildly sad, mood. When you are in a funk, sort of a melancholy feeling stretched out over time, you look for reasons to become sad; you are always ready to move to a feeling of sadness. I want to remind you that your rational brain has little to do with this movement from a melancholy mood to a feeling of sadness. This is not a conscious move. It is an emotional one.

If you are in a contemptuous mood you are quicker to feel disgust and disdain. When you are in a manic mood (i.e., euphoric), you are predisposed to feel pleasure, excitement and exhilaration.

Temperament is your "biologically based emotional disposition."[13] Temperament is measured in years or decades. Frequently, your temperament remains the same throughout your entire lifespan. We now know that you can learn how to change your temperament to one of greater optimism which has huge benefits on a number of levels. I'll speak to this more in a later chapter.

In summary, emotions are short-term, immediate affect (feelings). Moods are your mid-term feeling states. And temperament is your long-term feeling state. Temperament predisposes you to certain moods and emotions. Moods predispose you towards particular emotions.

How Wide is the Net of Affect Cast?

The second difference between emotions, moods and temperament has to do with how widely the net of affect is spread. Emotions "belong" to a specific action, situation, remark or person. When you get emotional, you can usually look for, and find, a particular reason why you became emotional.

For example, when you get mad at a friend due to his insensitive remark, you are angry with him and him only. Your anger is directed at your friend. You are not angry with your mother or your sister or anyone or anything else. You are only angry at the friend who insulted you. The "net" of affect, your anger, is only spread over your friend.

So emotions are directed at a particular person or situation. Most times, you are able to tell that a feeling is attached to a certain situation or person.

On the other hand, moods and temperament are much more diffuse. Moods influence nearly everything around you - the quality of your relationships, your performance at work, in sports and at home (see Figure 9). When you are irritable (in an angry mood), you tend to be impatient with your brother, your spouse, your children, nearly everyone around you. While you may be able to put on a happier face for work, the irritation rears up again once you return home, exhausted, from work.

Emotions are related to a single event. Moods are more diffuse and spill over into more areas of life. Temperament colors the way in which you perceive the entire world.

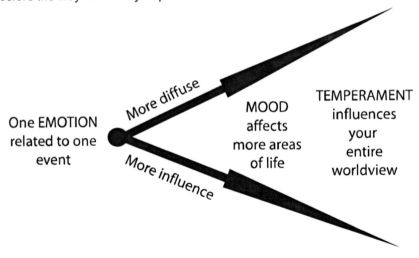

Figure 9. Diffusion of Affect

Moods are not connected to a certain individual or singular event. Moods come over you. They are not connected to a specific event.

In the same manner, temperament affects your entire worldview. If you have a negative temperament (i.e., a pessimistic outlook), you interpret events, actions, and verbal and nonverbal cues in a negative manner. You look for and find the worst in people.

How Old is the Notion of Emotional Intelligence?

Plato started the conversation about the importance of emotional intelligence over 2,000 years ago when he wrote, "All learning has an emotional base."

If you have a positive temperament (i.e., an optimistic outlook), you view the world around you with more grace, forgiveness, and gratitude. You look for and find the best in people and events. Your temperament influences your perception of everything around you. The "net" of temperament is widely cast and covers everything in your life.

Causes of Emotions, Moods and Temperament

The other way in which a mood is different from an emotion is that when you have an emotion, you can usually say what caused it, what brought the feelings forth. With a mood, we often cannot say what created it. We can simply wake up in a lousy mood for no known reason. Moods are produced by internal changes that do not relate to what is happening to us externally. Moods just seem to happen.

Temperament is similar to moods in that there is no identifiable cause for it. Your genetic make-up and early environment determine the vast majority of your temperament. Temperament isn't attached to anything that we can readily identify. You have a negative or positive temperament regardless of insults, compliments, weather, lifestyle or quality of relationships. Temperament dramatically influences how you perceive the world around you. It is the lens through which you see the world. I'll talk about this more in later chapters.

Thus, emotions, moods and temperament differ in terms of how quickly they come over you, how long they stick around, how diffuse they are, and whether or not they have an identifiable cause.

The Analogy of a Broadway Play

An analogy to help you understand the relationship between emotions, moods and temperament is that of a theater play. If you think of your emotional life as a play on Broadway, your temperament is the large screen backdrop that serves as the background for the entire first act or the entire play. The backdrop separates the front of the stage, where the play takes place, from backstage, and the area where many activities are happening at a rapid pace to create the illusion of reality out on stage.

Moods are the individual elements of scenery that are rolled on and off the stage with each scene. The scenic elements "set the stage" for the scene. The scenic elements may create an ominous and scary setting. Or they may create a peaceful, sunny and relaxed environment. The scenic elements change every act and may change many times during the course of the play.

Emotions are the actors that move quickly around the stage, speaking in short and energetic bursts. Each of the actors temporarily acts out the role of an emotion such as anger, surprise, or contentment. The actors can embody emotions that are positive, negative or neutral.

Everyone wears an emotional mask at times. In some cases, the face behind the mask (your true self) can be quite frightening.

Emotional Masks

There is one other aspect of the emotional landscape that is relevant here because it plays such a huge part in how we interact with other people in our daily life. The way you feel on the inside may differ from the "brave face" that you show to the outside world. *"Emotional mask"* is the phrase I use to describe the feelings that you convey to others via *conscious* manipulation of your facial expressions and body language. It's how we want other people to believe that we are feeling.

For example, when I was younger, I frequently felt fearful inside, yet as I became more and more skilled in hiding it, no one would have ever guessed that I was fearful unless I told them. The emotional mask I presented was one of calm control despite feeling afraid much of the time.

Research done by Paul Ekman at UCSF has shown that, despite our best conscious efforts to manage our expressions, all of us experience a phenomenon known as "emotional leakage."[14] Ekman notes that one form of emotional leakage is "microexpressions" which are incredibly quick facial expressions that last less than two-tenths of a second. These microexpressions reveal what you are truly feeling despite your attempts to conceal it.

These false expressions are given away by the fact that they are somewhat asymmetrical (i.e., the expression on one half of the face differs from the other half) and they are abrupt and unnatural in how they flow on and off the face.

The important thing to remember here is that the expression others wear on their face is not always a true account of how they really feel. Yet, with practice and awareness, you can learn to discover what people are truly feeling by tuning into their microexpressions.

Back to Emotional Mastery - Emotional Awareness

Let's return to the level of your emotions to discuss emotional mastery in more detail. Emotions occur instinctively within the body, regardless of your level of awareness, stimulation or intelligence. Emotions are necessary for homeostasis, or balance. Emotions mark a departure from homeostasis and they motivate us to act to restore balance. They are a push towards self-healing. Emotions are the "noises" of your body doing its routine work. They come to your awareness only when your balance is upset.

The problem is that if you are unaware of your emotions, then you are at their mercy. If you are at the mercy of your emotions, your health is at risk. An inability to manage your negative emotions leads to greater perceived bodily pain, slower recovery from surgery, increased blood pressure, cardiovascular problems, weakened immune system, more frequent illness, and greater likelihood of mental disorders. [15,16,17,18,19,20,21,22]

Yet with slight effort and practice, many previously unperceived emotions can be made conscious. In addition, you can learn to reduce the intensity and duration of many negative emotions, such as anger and fear. The ultimate goal is to learn to *manage* your emotions, so that your emotions don't manage you.

Sadness gives you time to reflect, re-energize and grieve after the loss of a loved one, the loss of a dream or a relationship.

At this point, I want to bring up an important difference between emotional management and emotional control. Emotional control is impossible, unhealthy and undesirable. You cannot control when and where your emotions are triggered. Nor do you want to. Each of your emotions serves a critical purpose.

Fear acts to keep you safe.

Anger motivates you to act to move barriers preventing you from reaching your goals.

Anger can also spur you to act in the service of social justice and equality.

Sadness works to keep you safely close to home and pull in social resources during a time of loss.

Emotional control is an either/or proposition: You either control your emotions or you don't.

On the other hand, the skill of emotional management looks at each emotion as existing on a continuum. Each emotion exists to varying degrees. Take the emotion of anger, for instance. Think of anger on a scale of 1 through 10 where 1 is mildly irritated, 5 is somewhat angry and 10 is highly enraged. The idea of emotional management is not to eliminate anger (or any other emotion) completely. The idea is to become aware of your anger as soon as it comes over you, to interrupt the anger cycle, and to have a choice as to how to proceed. The idea is to get to a place where you have a choice over how you respond to emotionally charged situations.

Emotional management is the skill of turning down the intensity and duration of your negative emotions. Emotional management allows you to have more of a conscious choice in which emotions you feel and to what degree. It's my belief, based on twenty years of studying emotions, that emotional management is one of the most important goals you can strive for in this lifetime.

As you become more aware of the bodily sensations of each of your emotions; as you learn to respond to them more appropriately, you will begin to respond in more and more appropriate manners.

The best emotional responses allow you to quickly achieve your goal, while causing no harm to others who may be involved. Obviously, this is not an easy skill to acquire. If it were, everyone would have it down. Yet, with awareness and practice, emotional management can become an invaluable skill on your path to success and happiness.

Emotions as Action Scripts

Before we move into the particulars of each emotion, allow me to share a deeper understanding of how emotions operate in general. Emotions are best understood as action scripts that have multiple components and occur over a relatively short period of time.

The action script of an emotion plays out like this: An emotion is triggered by an event that requires your mind to interpret the event. This interpretation may be conscious or unconscious. In other words, you may be aware of it; you may not. The interpretation of the event sets off a cascade of tendencies such as an inner, subjective experience (the "feeling" part inside you), facial expression, bodily changes, and relevant thoughts. This cascade of actions takes place in a fraction of a second.[23]

In general, an emotion includes the following:

1) A feeling that accompanies the emotion – that initial *rush* of feeling that precedes or occurs simultaneously with the initial thoughts (e.g, fear)

"Run AWAYYY!"

2) Thoughts – that follow quickly on the heels of the feeling (e.g., "I'm in danger.")

3) Internal bodily changes (e.g., increased heart rate and blood rushing to the hands) and

4) External bodily changes that accompany the feeling (e.g., facial expressions, perspiring palms, and perspiration).

Another Way to Look at the Emotional Action Script...

1. Emotional trigger (e.g., bear approaching) →

  2. Automatic appraisal or interpretation (e.g., body is in danger) →

    3. Internal bodily changes (e.g., heart rate rises) →

      4. External bodily changes (e.g., open mouth, wide eyes) →

        5. Action (e.g., turn and run) →

          6. Emotional awareness (subjective experience of fear) →

            7. Thoughts based on feeling (e.g., "I'd better get the heck out of here!")

All of these changes typically occur within milliseconds of the preceding event. The aftereffects, such as muscle tension, may remain with you for some time, but the initial changes that accompany an emotion occur within one-third of a second.

Function of Positive Emotions

The primary function of positive emotion is to broaden and build. That is to say that positive emotion, such as joy and happiness, allows your mind to blossom, creating more options, more possibilities, in terms of thoughts and actions.[24] Positive emotions help us be more creative, imaginative, and innovative. If you need to brainstorm for a new marketing slogan, you'll do a better job if you are happy when you do it.

In addition, positive emotions have long-term beneficial effects because they "build enduring personal resources, which function as reserves to be drawn on to manage future threats."[25] In other words, positive emotions fill up your gas tank. This means that positive emotions fill your emotional reservoir, your gas tank, with positive emotional energy to increase your sense of well-being and physical health.

What's more, positive emotions have been shown to undo the lingering physiological effects of negative emotions.[26] In psychology, it is understood that bad is stronger than good, or the negative is stronger than the positive.[27] Bad events have a greater power over us, our emotions, thoughts and behaviors, than do good ones. You are more motivated to avoid bad self-definitions than to pursue good ones. You are quicker to form bad

> Bad events, thoughts and feelings are 3 to 5 times more powerful than good ones. So the goal is the inverse of this - to be happy three times more often than you are unhappy.

Three smiles beats one frown. The goal is three times as much happiness as sadness.

judgments of other people than good ones. It takes approximately 5 compliments to undo the negative effects from one insult. Your brain processes negative information more thoroughly than it does positive information. So it's great news that the harmful effects of negative feelings can be undone by positive emotions.

Three Layered Model of Temperament, Mood and Emotion

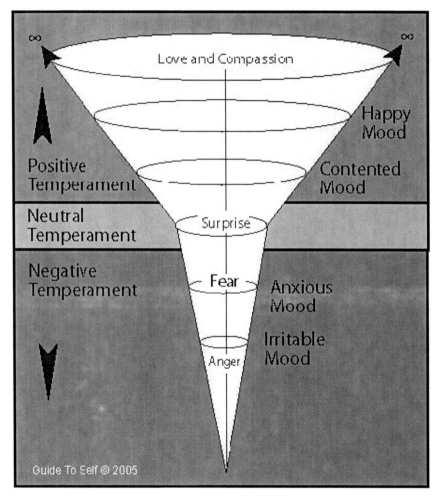

Figure 10. The Three Layered Model of Temperament, Mood and Emotion

Role of Neutral Emotions

The only neutral emotions are surprise and confusion. These two emotions serve as a signal to either yourself or the outside world that more information needs to be gathered prior to acting. Neutral emotions indicate that there is not enough information to reach a conclusion. Neutral emotions serve a useful function by helping us identify those times when more information is needed before you can act in an unwavering manner. Surprise and confusion tell us "Stop what you're doing. Get more data. You don't have enough info to figure out what is going on around you."

Function of Negative Emotions

The purpose of negative emotions is to narrow our focus and our possible reactions to perceived danger, threat and loss. Examples of negative emotions include contempt (or moral superiority), sadness, disgust, anger, fear, hatred, and shame to name but a few. Negative emotions were much more useful for our primal ancestors when a threat was usually life-threatening and hair trigger emotional responses saved you to live another day. In this day and age, however, our body mistakes a great number of trivial incidents

It's easy to get angry. Anger is contagious. You can catch anger from others. The hard part is finding ways to stay happy.

as truly life-threatening. This leads to a host of problems internally (e.g., release of cortisol, muscle tension, heart problems, etc.) and externally (e.g., impulsive emotional decisions that ruin relationships, cause wars, lead to physical confrontation and so on). We are better off to the extent that we reduce the amount of time that we spend under the mesmerizing spell of our negative, destructive emotions.

Each negative emotion has a different purpose. For instance, anger is a warning signal that something or someone has come between you and one of your goals.

Emotion and Perceptions

While there is still debate over whether a thought can exist without emotion, science has discovered that sensory perceptions *cannot* be separated from our emotions.[28] Emotion appears to be inextricably intertwined with the perceptions from our senses. The very act of perceiving the world is already filled with emotion. Perception cannot exist without emotion. Every perception we have is tinted by our feelings, moods and temperament. Even the act of separating out thought from emotion in this book is a false dichotomy. Truly there is no way to separate thought from feeling at this point in time. You can think of certain things in a logical, objective manner, such as a measuring tape. However, most thoughts cause or are a result of mood and emotion.

So to some extent we cannot rid ourselves completely of destructive emotions because both emotions and thoughts are hard wired into our brains. In particular, negative emotions arise naturally as a result of internal and external circumstances. In addition, negative moods do not need anything at all to start them off. A bad mood may begin merely as a function of the cycle of moods through which your body naturally progresses.

While you can reduce the frequency and intensity of negative emotions by changing your perceptions, you cannot do away with them completely; nor would you want to. However, you do want to become aware of them as soon as possible. Once you have recognized the emotion, you must understand the message the emotion is sending you.

Messages Sent by Emotions

Certain emotions convey certain messages thanks to millions of years of evolutionary programming. Here are the messages sent by each negative emotion in their simplest form.

Fear tells you to flee or freeze. Fear protects the body from physical harm and forces you to flee or freeze and blend in with the surroundings.

Anger arises when something gets in the way of you and your goal.

Sadness tells you when it is time to stay close to home where it is safer and friends are nearby.

Disgust warns you of something potentially poisonous or noxious.

As soon as you understand what the negative emotion is telling you, release the emotion using visualization, forgiveness and deep breathing. Use whatever tools are necessary to minimize the duration and intensity of the negative emotions. It's not that you want to eliminate negative emotions from your life completely. It's that you want to spend more of your time in positive emotions and moods.

Negative emotions cloud your perceptions and thinking in nearly all situations and you are better off to the extent that you release them as soon as you are aware of them.

This does NOT mean that you should repress your negative emotions or bury them. It does mean that you must develop the emotional awareness to recognize your feelings *in the moment* so that you can increase the options available to you. We'll discuss this in more detail later in this chapter.

Moods and emotions are the predispositions with which you meet reality. In the act of meeting reality, your perception is already influenced by your mood and emotions. Thus, it is more accurate to think of perception as intertwined with emotion. *The essential idea is that you must learn to foster more positive emotions while spending less time wallowing in negative emotions.*

Exercise - Daily Emotion Journal:

As emotions underlie every thought, perception and action you have, you want to learn to accurately identify which emotion you are feeling *as you are experiencing it.* Remember, it takes practice, repetition and awareness to tame your alligator – the emotional part of your mind.

One of the best ways to train your alligator, or your wild stallion, is to teach yourself to become more aware of what you are feeling and why. The best method I know of to do this is to use the Daily Emotion Journal below to increase your awareness of what you feel, what you think and the event or person that triggered the thoughts and feelings.  When you feel an emotion coming on, ask yourself, "What do I notice happening within my body?" and "What happened right before this emotion to possibly trigger it?" Simply jot down your emotions, moods, thoughts, triggers and responses at the end of each day. I have provided a copy of the journal for you to use below.

How to Use the Daily Emotion Journal

At the end of each day, write down the date and the time that the emotion reared up in the first column. This is helpful in uncovering patterns in your emotions and moods. It may be that you get irritable towards the end of the weekend which leads to anger and frustration Sunday evening and Monday mornings. Or perhaps you go into a funk towards the end of each month when money gets scarce which predisposes you towards emotions of sadness.

Second, describe the upsetting event or person that triggered the emotion. What was going on? Did your friend say something hurtful? Did your son miss a lunch date with you? Was your boss condescending? Were you exhausted? Stressed out? Describe the situation just before the emotion as best you can. This will help you understand what situations and which people trigger certain emotions in you.

Daily Emotion Journal

Date and Time	Describe the Trigger/ Event	Emotion	Degree of Emotion 1– 100 scale Mild to Extreme	Mood	Thoughts	Your Response

Third, write down the emotion, or emotions, you felt during the situation. The following is a list of feeling words which is meant as a starting point for you to begin the process of emotional self-discovery. It is not intended to be exhaustive or definitive. It is a list to brainstorm how you may be feeling. In my opinion, one of the reasons that emotional awareness is a rare skill to find in people is because we lack the language to describe it. As you develop the language to talk specifically and correctly about emotions, you will become better able to understand, connect to and resonate with other people in your life. Families of emotions are listed in bold type with related emotions placed beneath each one. So if you are feeling angry, yet "anger" doesn't adequately define how you feel, simply look under the category of anger to find a better description. Some of the words are repeated under separate emotional families as they apply to more than one family (e.g., "dislike" is under "contempt" as well as "disgust"). These are merely possible emotions that you may experience. Not all of them meet the scientific criteria for emotions.

Fourth, note down how intense the emotion was on a scale of 1 to 100 where 1 is minimal and 100 is very, very powerful. Write down how hard the emotion hit you so you have an idea of relative improvement over time. You are looking for little, tiny steps of improvement. Improvement can be either in terms of how frequently you are overtaken by a particular emotion, how intense the emotion is when it overtakes you and how long the emotion stays with you. So an improvement may be reducing the intensity of your anger when you do get angry. Another sign of improvement is that you become angry less often. And the last sign of improvement to look for is a reduction in the amount of time it takes you to release the negative emotion. For example, let's say when you begin this exercise that when you get sad, you stay sad for seven days on average. Over time, you will find that it will become easier to shake off your sadness and perhaps the sadness only stays with you for 5 days. And then 3 days. And then 1 day. And then 12 hours. And so on.

Next, jot down what mood you think you were in prior to the emotion hitting you. You may not be able to tell the difference between your mood and your emotion at first. Just keep bringing the difference to your conscious awareness. Emotions are the short-term feeling state (seconds to minutes). Mood is the mid-term feeling state (days to weeks).

After that, write down what thoughts you had just before or during the emotional event. There is no right or wrong here. Just write down the thoughts that cross the screen of your mind which lies just behind your forehead. I'll go into the different types of Gremlin thinking and how to challenge them later on.

Finally, note down your response to the situation. What did you do as a result of the event or the emotion? Did you say something hurtful? Did you lash out in anger? Did you withdraw in fear? Maybe you didn't do a thing? Whatever you did, note it down in the last column.

As you follow this procedure for a few months, you'll begin to see patterns emerge. These patterns are your alligator. With practice, awareness and intention, you'll begin to tame the atavistic alligator so he cooperates much more often with your alligator trainer (i.e., the conscious, rational part of your mind).

A Partial List of Emotions

Angry	Contempt	Disgust	Excited	Fearful
Aggravated	Abhorrence	Appalled	Amazed	Afraid
Angry at self	Animosity	Averse	Animated	Agitated
Angry at other	Appalled	Dislike	Anticipating	Anxious
Annoyed	Cruel	Disturbed	Ardent	Apprehensive
Bothered	Derisive	Horrified	Aroused	Distressed
Bugged	Detest	Loathing	Delighted	Dread
Burned up	Disdain	Nauseated	Eager	Edgy
Caustic	Disgrace	Noxious	Elated	Inhibited
Cranky	Dislike	Offended	Electrified	Irritated
Disappointed	Hate	Put off	Empowered	Fidgety
(sadness + anger)	Horrified	Repulsed	Energetic	Fragile
Dismayed	Hostile	Repugnant	Energized	Frazzled
Disgruntled	Loathing	Revulsion	Enthused	Frightened
Displeased	Scornful		Enthusiastic	Helpless
Enraged			Exhilarated	Insecure
Exasperated		**Tired**	Fired Up	Jittery
Explosive	**Confused**		Inflamed	Jumpy
Frustrated		Beat	Invigorated	Mistrustful
Furious	Addled	Bushed	Lively	Nervous
Impatient	Ambivalent	Burned out	Passionate	Overwhelmed
Incensed	Baffled	Depleted	Playful	Panicked
Indignant	Bewildered	Dog-tired	Rambunctious	Petrified
Irritated	Dazed	Enervated	Roused	Restless
Irate	Flustered	Exhausted	Stimulated	Scared
Irked	Hesitant	Fatigued	Thrilled	Shaky
Livid	Lost	Lethargic	Titillated	Stressed out
Mad	Muddled	Listless	Vibrant	Suspicious
Outraged	Mystified	Pooped		Terrified
Pissed off	Perplexed	Sleepy		Threatened
Rageful	Puzzled	Tuckered out		Uncertain
Resentful	Stumped	Weary		Wary
	Torn	Wiped out		
	Unsettled	Worn out		Worried
Guilty	Happy	Joyous	Surprised	Sad

Ashamed	Amused	Affirmed	Amaze	Abandoned
Chagrined	Calm	Appreciated	Astonish	Alone
Contrite	Content	Blissful	Astound	Apathetic
Culpable	Cheerful	Cheerful	Awe	Beaten
Degrade	Comfortable	Connected	Confound	Castrated
Disgrace	Compassionate	Content	Dazzle	Depressed
Dishonor	Competent	Eager	Dumbfound	Dejected
Embarrassed	Confident	Ecstatic	Flabbergast	Despair
Flustered	Congruent	Elated	Incredulous	Despondent
Humiliated	Delighted	Enthralled	Shock	Devastated
Immoral	Eager	Exuberant	Stagger	Disappointed
Mortified	Energetic	Gifted	Startle	Discouraged
Regretful	Friendly	Grateful	Stun	Disheartened
Remorseful	Generous	Gratified	Stupefy	Distraught
Self-loathing	Genuine	Healed	Taken aback	Forlorn
Self-conscious	Giddy	Hopeful	Wonder	Gloomy
Shame	Glad	Loved		Grief
Sheepish	Gracious	Peaceful		Heartbroken
Sinful	Invigorated	Radiant		Heavy hearted
Stigmatized	Jubilant	Rapturous		Hopeless
Worthless	Lively	Reverence		Hurt
	Passionate	Secure		Inconsolable
	Peaceful	Sincere		Isolated
	Pleased	Thrilled		Lonely
	Relaxed	Understood		Melancholic
	Rested	Useful		Miserable
	Synchronous	Whole		Regretful
	Tickled	Wonderful		Unhappy
	Vibrant	Worthy		Useless
	Warm			Wretched

> *Self-conquest is really self-surrender. Yet before we can surrender ourselves, we must become ourselves. For no one can give up what he does not possess.*
> *Thomas Merton*

More exercises to help tame your emotional alligator will follow later in this book. For now, I will turn to the reasons that we have positive, negative and neutral emotions.

The Major Positive Emotions Happiness and Joy

Happiness improves your ability to think and act by encouraging you to push through limits, creating the urge to play, and approaching problems from innovative ways.[29] This increase in your potential thoughts and actions builds positive emotional energy reservoirs that can be used at a later time to help you cope with stressful events. In other words, *happiness fills your reservoir with positive energy.*

Happiness puts a stop to the mental processes that create anxious and fearful thoughts. There are no other recognizable bodily responses except for a peaceful serenity, which also fills your energy reservoir to help you heal and thrive. When you are happy, you are less focused on your self, enjoy others more and want to share your good experience with others.

Happiness creates a readiness and enthusiasm for the task at hand and for working towards constructive goals, such as socializing and exercising. When you are happy, your brain discourages negative feelings and thoughts and allows for an increase in your energy.[30]

Physiological Cues of Happiness

There are two types of smiles: the "Duchenne smile" and the inauthentic smile. The "Duchenne" smile is the "real" smile. It takes action by two muscles to create a full smile, the cheeks and the muscles above the eyes (the orbicularis oculi). The false smile is noticeable as the individual does not use the major muscle above the eyes. The false smile only uses the cheek muscles to create the smile giving the impression of a pleasant yet impatient smile.

Gratitude

Gratitude reduces heart rate variability, increases immune system functioning and opens up the possible array of thoughts and actions. Gratitude adds meaning to normal actions.[31],[32]

A life directed by gratefulness is the panacea for unending yearnings, desires and life's ills. Gratitude leads to peace of mind, happiness, physical health and deeper more satisfying relationships. It has been conceptualized as an emotion, attitude, trait, virtue, mood and coping response.[33]

The word "gratitude" derives from the Latin word root, "gratia," meaning grace, graciousness or gratefulness. All derivatives from this root have to do with kindness, generousness, gifts, the beauty of giving and receiving or getting something for nothing.

The object of gratitude is directed at something other than your self and could be people or something impersonal (e.g., nature) or something nonhuman (e.g., God, animals, cosmos). Gratitude stems from a perception of a positive personal outcome, which is not necessarily deserved or earned, that is due to the actions of another.

Gratitude is defined as a perceived benefit combined with the judgment that someone, or something, else is responsible for that gain. The benefit may be material or nonmaterial (emotional or spiritual). The central theme is the recognition of an altruistic gift. Gratitude is a complex state that requires both emotional and cognitive energy (i.e., thought). Gratitude is most similar to thankfulness at one end of the scale and most dissimilar to contempt, hate and jealousy. This ability to notice, appreciate and savor the elements of one's life has been viewed as a crucial determinant of well-being (Bryant 1989; Langston 1994).

Frijda (1988) said that "adaptation to satisfaction can be counteracted by constantly being aware of how fortunate one's condition is and how it could have been otherwise, or actually was otherwise before...enduring happiness seems possible and can be understood theoretically. The personal commitment to invest psychic energy in developing a personal schema, or worldview, of one's life as a "gift" or one's self as being gifted holds considerable sway from the standpoint of achieving optimal psychological functioning (Emmons & McCullough, 2003).

Love

Love, perhaps the highest of all emotions, engenders tender feelings and a sensual satisfaction. Love sets up your body to relax and lowers your defenses. The emotion of love results in a general state of calm, relaxation, contentment and an increased ability to work peacefully with others.

We are inundated with ideas about love some correct and some not so much. We are constantly bombarded by our culture, popular music, media and people around us with their ideas of what love should and should not be. As an example, Thomas Scheff, an eminent sociologist from UC Santa Barbara, found that over the past 30 years, roughly 25% of pop music songs in the Top 40 are about love gone bad or heartbreak. Scheff found that another 10% of the Top 40 songs have been about infatuation or love's longing. And another 10% of the most popular songs were about requited love. Finally, there were another 25% of the Top 40 songs which involved miscellaneous types of romantic love. *Only 25% of the Top 40 songs in the past thirty years* had nothing to do with love or romance! Yet, none of these popular renditions – infatuation, unrequited or requited love – truly suggest real, authentic love.

According to the bible of human strengths, *Character Strengths and Virtues: A Handbook and Classification,* by Christopher Peterson and Martin Seligman, there are three prototypical types of love: romantic love, a child's love for a parent and a parent's love for a child.

Romantic love involves passion, the desire for sexual, physical and emotional intimacy with another person whom makes you feel unique and special and who you make feel likewise.

A child's love for his or her parent is expressed as affection for their primary caregiver(s) who offer them affection, protection and emotional support. This love serves to keep the child close to the caregiver and provides them with a sense of safety and security from which they may venture out and explore the world.

The parent's love for a child involves comfort, protection, assistance and support of the child. Parental love involves self-sacrifice for the benefit of the child. Parental love means feeling truly happy when the child feels happy.

Relationships may involve more than one form of love. For example, best friends can love each other in a child to parent manner as well as in a parent to child manner. Best friends who love one another support each other emotionally, physically, spiritually and mentally. They protect one another similar to the love of a parent. And they provide a source of affection, protection and support just like the love of a child for a parent.

Relationships may also involve different forms of love at different points in time. For instance, dating couples may start off with romantic love involving passion and the burning desire to be intimate on a number of levels. Assuming the couple stays together long enough, the passion wanes and is largely replaced by the other two forms of love – parent to child and child to parent.[34]

Each of these three forms of love is slightly different but has similar core elements. Love is best viewed as an amalgam of distinctive positive emotions such as joy, interest, contentment and happiness which is experienced within the boundaries of safe, closer relationships. Love broadens our thinking and potential actions by creating recurring cycles of urges to play with, explore, and savor experiences with loved ones.

Example: When I fell in love with my wife, roughly 20 years ago, I felt like I was walking on clouds. I was euphoric and happy most of the time for 3-5 weeks. I lost all sense of time. While I had many, many things to do at the time, such as soccer practice, student body president duties, and studying, all I wanted to do was be with her. I just wanted to be next to her, talk to her, and smell her perfume. When I was away from her, all I could think about was our next meeting. I felt I had discovered someone to whom I could honestly talk. I wanted to bear my soul to her. I desired to protect her and comfort her.

Over time, however, the feeling of passion that exists in the beginning of a romantic relationship slowly fades away, not completely, but the intensity of the passion wanes. As months fade into years, the love of friendship grows, as if to replace the ebbing passion. While the desire for sexual, physical and emotional closeness remains, albeit at a more realistic level, feelings of affection, protection, self-sacrifice, empathy and trust grow stronger.

Physiological Cues of Love

People in love lean forward (posture) while displaying a coherent pattern of smiling, gazing at one another, and assuming open postures towards one another.

Capitalizing on Love

One of the foremost researchers in the area of love and marriage is Shelly Gable, an assistant professor of psychology at UCLA. Most researchers looking at marriage work on conflict management, how to create more harmony between partners, and how individuals in a couple cope with traumatic events. Gable is one of a handful of researcher who looks at what makes a thriving marriage. Her work provides some valuable insights if you are interested in transforming your good relationship (e.g., friendship, marriage, parent or child) into a great one.

Gable looks to see how you respond when your spouse tells you that he's just been promoted, or your child tells you that she won Class President, or when your mother tells you she won a tennis tournament, or when your friend tells you she just won a huge lawsuit. Gable puts your responses into four different categories which break down as follows:

1. An enthusiastic reaction such as "Wow! That's tremendous. That's the best thing I've heard all week. I'm sure there are more great things to come for you. You've definitely earned it. Congratulations!" This reaction is called the **active-constructive** response by Gable.
2. A more subdued reaction where you share your happiness but say little. For example, "That's nice dear." This is the **passive-constructive** response.
3. Or perhaps you point out some of the potential pitfalls or negatives within the good event. For instance, "Wow, I sure hope you can handle all that extra responsibility. Does this mean you will have to work extra hours?" Gable refers to this as the **active-destructive** response.
4. Or, you might respond with disinterest and not respond to the good news at all. Most folks do this by merely changing the subject, "Yes, but what do you think about the weather outside?" This is known as the **passive-destructive** response.

The first type of response, the active-constructive one, is called "capitalizing" by Gable and here's the fascinating part...*capitalizing amplifies the pleasure of the good event and creates an upward spiral of good feelings.*

Gable has shown that capitalizing is one of the keys to strong, supportive, thriving relationships.[35] So how do you respond to good news from other people? Are you a "capitalizer" who creates upward spirals of positive emotions? Or do you turn a blind eye and a deaf ear to the good news of others?

The consequences of learning how to be more of a "capitalizer" are impressive and robust. Couples who describe themselves as having a spouse who is active and constructive in response to their good news are:

- More committed to the relationship
- More in love
- Happier in their marriage

Think about that the next time your mate comes in the door with exciting news!

Specifics on the Major Negative Emotions

 In this chapter, I will cover the latest scientific information for each one of the negative emotions. Keep in mind that the term "negative" does not mean that these emotions are to be repressed or avoided. The main thing to remember about negative emotions is that each one serves a purpose. Your job is to recognize the emotion, understand the message it's sending, act on the message and then release the emotion via deep breathing and visualization which I'll cover more in a later chapter.

As you read through this section on negative emotions, recall the metaphor of the person wrestling an alligator. The "Crocodile Hunter" is like your rational, conscious part of your mind. The wild alligator is like your emotional, unconscious part of your mind. This whole section on negative emotions is critical information about your alligator. You have to be intimately familiar with your alligator if you want to tame it. I am primarily concerned with familiarizing you with the dark side of the alligator -- sadness, anger, fear, shame, guilt, and embarrassment.

Your job is to learn to identify each one of these emotions in a split second. As this is difficult when you first start out, you may want to begin by dividing up your thoughts and actions as based in one of two primary emotions – love or fear. Before you act, simply act yourself, "Is this an act of love or an act of fear?" You can also think to yourself, "Are my thoughts fueled by love or by fear?" Once you get the love-fear dichotomy down, then you are ready to move on to advanced discernment of the full emotional spectrum.

So let's get going with fear…

Fear

The vast majority of us go through life afraid. The source of the fear may vary. All of us are scared of something and, when we're afraid, we are absolutely ruled by fear. Too many of us don't realize our potential because we are afraid - afraid of people, afraid of what others will think, afraid of our own feelings, afraid of asking for help, and so on. *Do not settle for a life filled with fear.* At the simplest level, there are two basic motivators of human behavior – fear and love. If you are not acting out of love, you are acting out of fear.

What follows is a powerful description of fear (and the battle of Fallujah) from Spc. John Brady, a 23-year-old infantryman with the Army's First Infantry Division Task Force 2/2 in Iraq:

> "It was warm in the Bradley (armored vehicle) at night, but the darkness would drive you crazy. Being in there for so long, you start to claw at the walls and lose your sense of time...then the ramp drops and you are forced into the world again, like a crying, naked, cold, frightened newborn being forced from the womb, having to learn everything about the world in a matter of seconds. It is all primitive instinct and soldier instinct at points like that in the fight. And it's horrible. I ...hate those feelings, when you don't know where you are, where you are taking fire from, where all your people are or where you are going. Everything is exploding: bullets and tracers are going in both directions at and away from you. And in these moments, you lose yourself and turn into a robot, only able to think about the other robots around you and the hate that consumes the only part of your soul still left hinged and intact. Hate and fear fuel your desire to kill, soldiering enables you to take that emotional part and transfer it into action, ordered and neat...It's almost beautiful at times what soldiers are capable of doing when you don't have any other choice than to fight or die. Fear is always there. And we do get all (messed) up, and (things) go wrong and nothing turns out right, but you have to just keep overcoming, in some way or another. I don't really know how it happens, but it does. Thinking back on it, it

never seemed like it was "me" that was there. Like I was watching it from the outside. But the fear was there, so it must have been real."[36]

Figure 11. The Physiological Clues to Fear

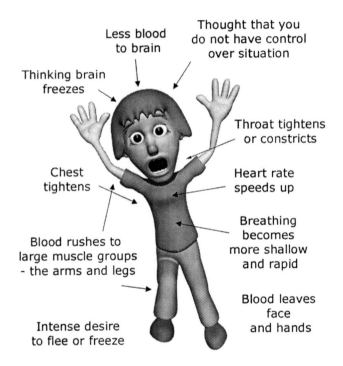

Bodily Cues of Fear

Less blood to brain

Thought that you do not have control over situation

Thinking brain freezes

Throat tightens or constricts

Chest tightens

Heart rate speeds up

Breathing becomes more shallow and rapid

Blood rushes to large muscle groups - the arms and legs

Blood leaves face and hands

Intense desire to flee or freeze

Physiological Cues of Fear

As illustrated by Spc. Brady's description, fear follows a perception of immediate, concrete and overwhelming physical danger. As seen in Figure 11, fear occurs when you believe that you are not in control, either physically or emotionally. When you are afraid, your blood gathers in the large skeletal muscles such as those in your arms and legs, preparing your body to flee. The physiological cues of fear include a quickening of breathing, a tightening of the throat, tightness in the chest, perspiration, difficulty breathing, quickened heart rate, a feeling of wanting to flee (or freeze), and reduced blood flow to the brain.

Blood leaves your face thereby making you appear paler and in some cases blotchy. Your body freezes for a moment to gauge your possible reactions such as what is the quickest escape route. The worst part of fear is the brain freeze that accompanies the bodily changes. When fear sets in, the alligator wrestler, the thinking side of your mind, is paralyzed and unable to respond. As a result, you get tongue-tied, lose all ability to think straight, are unable to answer questions and think. This is what happens in people who have performance anxiety, social anxiety, and phobias. Their mind is set to signal fear quickly and easily. Once the fear response is sounded, the thinking mind becomes nearly useless. At that point, you are responding in a primitive animalistic mode. At that point, the alligator reigns supreme.

You want to be aware of these cues in order to decrease the time it takes you to consciously recognize what emotion is overtaking you. The goal is to identify the emotion, honor it, breathe through it and eventually release it as quickly as possible.

Fear is the equivalent of a "brain fart." Fear paralyzes your thinking mind.

Accompanying the chemical changes in the brain is an overwhelming flood of anxious thoughts which are seemingly uncontrollable. This intense cycle of fear and worry often paralyzes the individual in a figurative sense. It also paralyzes the rational mind, making it unable to think clearly.

Fear and anxiety are closely linked. Fear is the momentary emotion while anxiety is the longer-term mood. If the fear is held onto (and not released), the brain moves towards long-term anxiety, forcing the brain to focus repeatedly on the perceived threat. The anxious mind begins an endless spiral of negative thoughts, feelings and chemical reactions. Fear-based worrying lies at the heart of all anxiety.

Courage as the Antidote to Fear

Courage is the antidote to fear. Courage is not the absence of fear but the exorcising of it. You need to feel the fear, breathe it out and push through it. It is the conquering of your fears that makes one brave. One cannot be brave without fear. This step involves taking concrete actions to help us achieve our dreams. By reframing the question as, "What am I willing to try?" you can make change exciting, rather than paralyzing. Whenever you feel fearful, find out what it is that is making you feel that way. Then, go after the fear-inducing situation in small, manageable steps.

I was afraid to try soccer at first. Twelve years later, I was captain of my high school varsity soccer team.

Example: I used to have a fear of speaking in public. I figured out that my fear was holding me back personally and professionally. I decided to attack the fear by becoming president of a human resources organization. This forced me to speak in front of a crowd at least once a month. It also forced me to socialize with others which lead to other speaking engagements. After one year, I'm happy to report that my fear of public speaking is under control. I'm currently doing a daily talk show on the radio as well as regular public speaking engagements.

My greatest opponent is fear. I fear everything. As a result, I have been attacking my fears ever since I was very young. My first recollection of conquering fear occurred when I was five years old with the help of my mother. From my front window, I was watching some boys play soccer across the street. My mom recognized my desire to play and the fear that held me back. She pushed me out the door so I'd go play soccer with the older boys on the block. I reluctantly crossed the street and asked to play. They assigned me to a team. I ended up scoring my first goal that day. Success!

Genuine acts of courage do not happen on the spur of the moment even though it may appear that way. It appears that way because we do not have access to the inner life of the person who acts courageously. Such a person has had to work hard to develop courage. Typically, brave individuals live from the center of their heart, but not in a sentimental way. The courageous person is engaged and fully aware, yet not self-conscious.

Courage, as a way of being, reveals itself in thought and feeling as well as physical action. One's whole life can be an act of courage. It is not at all necessary to face an insurmountable obstacle to be courageous. The person, who lives life with clear goals and values, moving toward these step by step certainly falls into the category of courageous, provided the way is accompanied by the authentic experience of soul and spirit.

A slightly different way to look at it is that there is no such thing as failure. Failure is merely a judgment by which an action may be labeled. As opposed to judging yourself and others actions as successful or failures, replace failure with the thought that "There is no failure. There are only learning experiences." For it is far better to take the risk, act and produce results (good or bad) than to become numb by living in constant fear.

In addition, never label yourself or another individual a "failure". The distinction must be made between the singular act of failure, or learning experience, and being a failure. Just because you have failed, or had numerous learning experiences, in the past, does not make you a failure. There are no failures, merely people learning how to play the game of life.

When you do encounter the inevitable setback or make a mistake, ask yourself what you will do with the information you've learned about yourself as a result. Be grateful for the lessons given to you – the good and the bad. Every experience teaches us something.

Sadness

The main reason for sadness is to help you adjust to a significant loss, such as the death of a family member or loss of an old friend. Sadness is accompanied by a drop in energy level and enthusiasm for activities and play. As the sadness deepens and approaches depression, sadness slows your body down. This allows time to grieve, look inward at who you are and what you are doing with your life, and understand the meaning of the loss. Perhaps, most importantly, sadness keeps you close to home where you are safest, when you are vulnerable, after a loss or disappointment. After the sadness subsides, and your energy returns, you are able to plan for new beginnings.

Sadness is a temporary, fleeting emotion. Depression is a mood that lasts longer than two weeks. Sadness is cumulative. Sadness builds upon sadness. So if your first sad thought is followed by more sad thoughts, you risk a downward spiral.

For example, you may experience accumulated sadness if you are having a rough time at your job, more sadness due to trouble at home, and even more sadness due to the rainy weather. The more sad events you have in your life, the more sadness you will accumulate, *unless you learn how to release your sadness in the moment.*

Sadness is accompanied by a drop in your energy and enthusiasm for activities and play. It signals a desire to be comforted. As the sadness extends over time and approaches depression, your body slows down. Sadness keeps you close to home where you are safest, when you are vulnerable, after a loss or disappointment.

Chronic sadness has tremendous implications for your health. Some of the negative effects of sadness on your body include suppressed immune system functioning, clogging of arteries, loss of energy, muddled thinking, poor decision-making, and poor digestion.

Figure 12. The Physiological Clues to Sadness

Bodily Cues of Sadness

Inside corners of eyebrows turn upward

Tears welling up in your eyes

Lump in throat

Muddled thinking

Corners of your lips turn down

Perception of outer world becomes more negative

Fatigue or lack of energy

Desire to stay close to home

Inner dialogue becomes more and more negative

Physiological Cues of Sadness

Sadness is marked by feeling a lump in your throat, feeling tired, tears welling up in the eyes, the inner corner of the eyebrows turned upward, and dwelling on what or whom you are missing (see Figure 12). Each emotion has an action tendency which conditions your body to act in a certain way when that emotion arises. The action tendency of sadness is to make you feel like not doing anything. Sadness may induce crying which may cause others to provide things for you that you cannot, at that moment, attain for yourself. The goals of sadness include the desire to be comforted and the desire to recover something you've lost. With sadness, you do not necessarily feel like giving up (unlike depression). Sadness works to recover something passively by eliciting caring actions by other people.

The danger of both sadness and depression is that they slowly take over and dominate your perception of reality as well as your internal dialogue, the conversation that runs through your head. The sadness becomes your reality. Without realizing it, you begin to believe your own negative thoughts telling you that you are worthless, stupid and no good. Oftentimes, our negative emotions, especially sadness and irritability, are terribly insidious in that they creep in slowly and quietly. By the time you realize that you are dealing with sadness, it may have already significantly and negatively affected your perception of the world around you. In this scenario, we often don't even realize that our perceptions have changed, assuming that things have always been like this and always will be. This is dangerous. Many of my clients have spent their entire lives plodding through life weighted down by chronic negativity, irritability, and exhaustion. The problem is that they can't see it because they are so far immersed in their mood.

Non-stop irritability is one of the single best indicators of chronic sadness and anger. It's as if your emotional gas tank is filled to the top with sadness (often mixed up with anger), and any minor irritation is enough to make your gas tank overflow. The overflow shows up as irritation. The trick is to empty your gas tank of sadness and all other negative emotional energy and to refill it with positive emotional energy – happiness, gratitude, optimism, and joy.

If you suspect you may be irritable or sad a lot of the time, you are urged to take the Guide To Self Depression Screening at www.GuideToSelf. com and see your family doctor.

Happiness as the Antidote to Sadness

While it may seem obvious to say that happiness is the antidote to sadness, using happiness as the antidote to sadness is far easier said than done. The quickest path out of sadness is as follows:

1.) Become aware of the bodily sensations of sadness.
2.) Visualize breathing in happiness and breathing out sadness.
3.) Think thoughts about a time when you very happy (or imagine a made-up situation in which you are happy).

The first step is to become aware of the bodily sensations of sadness. These sensations include

1.) A feeling of tears welling up in your eyes,
2.) The corners of your lips turning down
3.) The inside corners of your eyebrows rising up
4.) Shallow breathing
5.) Feeling a lump in your throat
6.) A decrease in energy

Many times, we are so "numb" from years of ignoring these sensations that we cannot accurately identify these bodily cues. This is where the breathing exercises come in very handy. The foundation of all emotional awareness is deep breathing. To effectively manage your negative emotions, you must first slow down and become aware of the clues your body gives you every second of every day. As emotional management is the cornerstone of a successful and happy life, it must become one of your top priorities. The key to controlling sadness is to **interrupt the thought process** that fuels the sadness in the first place. Once you recognize that you are feeling sad, give yourself permission to feel the sadness. Keep in mind that emotions are just temporary. They will pass.

Second, once you are aware that you are beginning to feel sad, remind yourself to breathe deeply. When you get proficient at this process, it only takes a few deep breaths to rid yourself of the sadness. While breathing, imagine a white light filled with happiness pouring into your body when you inhale. And picture the sadness (as emotional energy) leaving your body as thick, black smoke when you exhale. Remember to exhale all the air out of your lungs to completely rid yourself of all sadness. Once you have identified the sadness and give it permission to exist, it's much easier to bring your awareness to your breathing and breathe the sadness out.

Finally, remember a time in the past when you were happy and hold that image in your mind. As an alternative, you can imagine a place of your own creation where you would be happy. I like to think of lying on a white sandy beach in the sun with waves gently running up the shore and warm air smelling of salt water.

Anger

Anger comes from the Latin word, *angere*, which means "to strangle." Anger strangles us on a number of different levels. It is the emotion which is probably the most familiar to the majority of us. A consistent finding in those who have low self-esteem, migraines, ulcers, heart attacks, substance abuse problems, troubled work and interpersonal relationships and frequent job loss is that they are unable to master their anger. Rather than controlling their anger, their anger controls them. While anger is not the sole cause of these problems, the constant appearance of anger in such individuals indicates that it is a prime factor in all of these problems.

Too much anger is toxic. Anger and hostility result in dis-ease of all types. It is physically arousing and has damaging physiological correlates, such as increased heart rate, more cortisol (a stress hormone) dumped into your system, muscle tension, headaches, decreased mental clarity and clogged arteries.

Anger signals the fact that something or someone has come between you and a desired goal of yours. It is a call to action. The goal may be as simple as trying to get home during rush hour. Yet, when another driver rudely cuts you off on the freeway, your anger rears its head.

The emotion anger is frequently confused with the actions you take while angry. This doesn't happen with fear. You don't confuse the emotion fear with the act of running away. However, anger is nearly always thought to be negative and destructive, despite the fact that anger itself is merely a feeling. Anger, in and of itself, if not acted upon, is instructive, not destructive. Anger can be a good thing. However, for anger to be positive, you must first learn to manage your emotions. Then you have a choice as to how to respond to anger's signal.

Four Types of Anger

To alleviate some of this confusion around anger, allow me to better acquaint you with the various types of anger. There are at least four types of anger of which we know: anger directed at self, anger directed at others, disappointment, and constructive anger.

1. Anger at Self

The first type is anger directed inwardly at oneself. The anger sits inside and burns and festers. After enough anger has been turned inward, it eventually leads to inappropriate angry outbursts at undeserving and unsuspecting people. Studies show that most people turn 90% of their anger inwards at themselves. Most of this anger is an attempt to control and contain the frightening emotion of anger. Anger can lead us to rage-filled, uncontrollable behaviors. Rather than feel the anger, honoring the feeling, and releasing it, most of us bottle it up. This stuffed anger is toxic and leads to all sorts of negative health outcomes. It also leads to displaced anger where you get angry with the wrong person, at the wrong time, and to the wrong degree.

2. Anger at Other

A second type of anger is directed outward. This type of anger builds upon itself and can frequently lead to rage. This form of outward-directed anger is typically displaced onto the wrong person, at the wrong time and in the wrong manner.

Both of the first two types of anger are destructive. Destructive anger includes anger that is directed inward and never released and anger that is inappropriately directed outward at others. Anger directed at others may be inappropriate in terms of its target (Are you directing your anger at the right person?), its intensity (Is the degree of anger in keeping with the offense?), its timing (Is this the best time to make your anger known?), and the manner in which it is communicated (Is this the best way to communicate my anger?).

It is extremely hard to get mad at the right person, to the right degree, at the right time and in the right manner.

3. Disappointment

The third type of anger exists in tandem with sadness and most closely resembles disappointment. Disappointment usually involves a judgment that has not been met. Judgments cause trouble for everyone. Judgments usually involve an element of moral superiority, as if you know what is best for someone else. Stay away from judgments.

4. Constructive Anger

The final type of anger is the type used as a positive motivator to act to remove an obstacle that is preventing you from reaching a goal. This type of anger can be a constructive anger, that is, an anger that is quickly released and prompts you to act in a positive manner to remove the obstacle from your path.

Constructive anger actually provides you with a persistent attitude which enables you to push forward to solve a given problem. These four types of anger have been demonstrated via several methods – reports from subjects in scientific studies, physiological evidence, and behavioral data.

When increasing your emotional awareness, part of the task is to learn the variety of subtle emotional differences within one family of emotion. The better equipped we are to make subtle differentiations within an emotion, such as anger, the better able you are to share with others the degree of feeling you are currently experiencing. With that in mind, let us turn to the bodily cues that anger provides us.

Bodily Cues of Anger

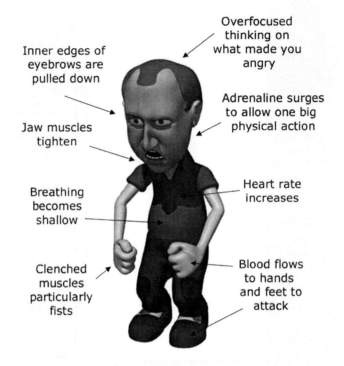

Inner edges of
eyebrows are
pulled down

Overfocused
thinking on
what made you
angry

Adrenaline surges
to allow one big
physical action

Jaw muscles
tighten

Heart rate
increases

Breathing
becomes
shallow

Clenched
muscles
particularly
fists

Blood flows
to hands
and feet to
attack

Figure 13. The Physiological Cues of Anger

Physiological Cues of Anger

Unmanaged anger will
lead to destructive outcomes
such as physical conflict.

In order to stop the cycle of anger, you have to tune in to the early warning signs. So pay attention! When you begin to feel angry, as seen in Figure 13, blood flows to your hands and feet, making it easier to strike at your perceived enemy, your heart rate increases, a rush of adrenaline kicks in and your body prepares for forceful action. Anger causes a surge of chemicals (catecholamines) which creates a quick, one-time rush of energy to allow for one brief shot at physical action. Meanwhile, in the background, another batch of chemicals, including cortisol, is released through the adrenocortical branch into the nervous system that creates a backdrop of physical readiness. This emotional undertone lasts much longer than the initial one-time surge and can last for days. This undertone keeps the brain in a special state of overarousal building a foundation on which reactions can occur with great speed.

Compassion as the Antidote to Anger

If you want to reduce your anger, think of the universe as compassionate and nurturing. As such it is designed to reward compassionate, nurturing behaviors in individuals. Compassion transcends both natural human sympathy and normal Christian concern, enabling one to sense in others a wide range of emotions and then provide a supportive foundation of caring. Compassion occurs when a person is moved by the suffering or distress of another, and by the desire to relieve it. Compassion is empathy, not sympathy. It is the identification with and the understanding of another's situation, feelings, and motives. This ability to put yourself in the other person's shoes serves as the perfect antidote to anger in which one perceives an obstruction to one's goals.

The goal is to understand the situation from the perspective of the other person. Often this involves interpreting the situation with a large degree of grace. For example, I am driving 75 miles per hour in the fast lane. A car comes up behind me doing 100 mph. The driver comes inches from my rear bumper in a desperate attempt to get me to move aside. At this point, my old interpretation was "That idiot! What does he think he's doing? I'm going 75! I'll show him." And then I let off the gas to slow down ever so slightly. My interpretation now is "He's probably trying to get to the emergency room. Perhaps there has been an accident." And I change lanes and let him by. No anger.

Steps to Managing Anger

The first step to mitigating anger is to become aware when you are feeling angry. The sooner you can identify the anger, the quicker you can take steps to honor it and release it. The trick is to interrupt the process of anger before it gets explosively out of hand. As soon as you feel yourself getting irritated, take a quick three-minute break and breathe deeply. When you get angry, your heart rate goes up. Breathing returns your heart rate and your emotional state to normal. This way, you are less likely to erupt in rage.

Ideally, anger is dealt with in the moment. You begin to get angry. You recognize your anger, label it and honor it. Tell yourself, "Okay, I'm feeling angry right now. That's okay. Breathe deeply. There is no reason to hold on to my anger. I am letting my anger pass through me." You breathe the anger out. If you can address your grievance with the other party, do so. Listen calmly to the other individual's side of the story. Work the misunderstanding through while letting go of your defensiveness. With practice, you can learn to stay calm, cool and collected in the midst of progressively difficult situations. Unfortunately, we can't always catch anger in the moment. To help you catch anger quickly and reduce the damage, here is an exercise:

First, identify the cause of your anger as quickly as possible. The most destructive type of anger is uncontrolled, impulsive, and unconscious. It can hurt you and others. When anger takes over, slow down. Remove yourself from the situation if possible. Identify the cause, but don't react. When you are angry, it is smart to stop speaking. Silence is the number one behavior to practice when you're mad. It shows you're in control of your anger. You also buy time to cool yourself down, breathe, and think of possible strategies to deal with the situation at hand.

If your anger is too great, get up and leave the room. Go somewhere else to give you time to cool off. Think about your anger on a ten point scale, where 1 is calm and 10 is full of rage. If your anger goes over 5 on the scale below, remove yourself from the situation until you and the other person are back in control emotionally.

Anger Scale

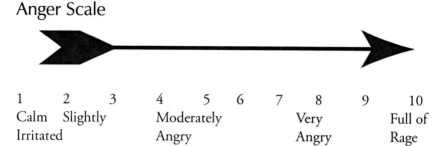

1	2	3	4	5	6	7	8	9	10
Calm	Slightly		Moderately				Very		Full of
	Irritated		Angry				Angry		Rage

Find creative and amusing ways to think about expressing your anger. For instance, think about photocopying your butt and sending an (anonymous) copy to the person who wronged you.

Second, allow yourself one to two days time to complain and vent your anger to others (who are not involved in the situation). *Do not bury, suppress or stuff your anger.* This will negatively impact your physical health. It also lends itself to the displacement of your anger onto other people who are not deserving of your wrath. Rather than repress your anger, honor it, label it, write it down in your journal, breathe it out, exercise, ponder on it, or discuss it with a coach or friend. This is helpful as it helps to dismantle the anger.

Third, after two days, make a conscious effort to release your anger. This means giving up on who is "right" and who is "wrong." Releasing your anger is a process, not a singular event. Anger gradually recedes over time. Anger is toxic. You do not want to hold onto it. To release your anger, breathe deeply and visualize your anger leaving your body as smoke with each exhalation. Remind yourself to breathe deeply occasionally throughout the day. It is also helpful to write down all of your anger in your journal. While writing, focus on each of the five senses as well as your thoughts, feelings and actions. Another useful tool to get rid of anger is prayer. Consciously giving up your anger to the universe via prayer is an effective way to relieve yourself of burdensome negative emotional energy.

Fourth, share your anger with the offending party *if* you believe that by sharing your anger your differences can be resolved. If your sense is that, by sharing your feelings you can improve the situation, then calmly express your point of view while attempting to stick to objective facts and "I" statements. "I" statements are statements that focus on how it makes you feel when someone else behaves a certain way. For example, "It makes me angry when you show up late for dinner." Your goal is to resolve the conflict. Your goal is not to make them pay for your suffering. Keep an open mind. Your statement may result in an apology from the offending party, a compromise, a negotiation, an agreement to disagree or nothing at all. Don't get pulled into a power struggle. Remain centered. Breathe deeply. And stand firm in the knowledge that you have shared the truth as you see it.

If the offending party is unreceptive, vindictive or apathetic, it may not be useful or constructive to share your feelings and the reasons behind them. In this case, repeat the first three steps to diffuse your anger. Take steps to distance yourself from the offending party, particularly if he or she is constantly negative. To the extent possible, reduce contact with the individual.

Another key to controlling anger is to interrupt the thought process that fuels the anger in the first place. As mentioned previously, you can reframe the situation in a more positive, gracious light. This works well to defuse the anger cycle.

Don't allow your thoughts to dwell in the gutter.
Dark thoughts prolong dark moods.

A powerful means to defuse anger is to distract yourself with something you find pleasant and enjoyable. It's hard to be angry when you're having a good time. Don't continue to dwell on thoughts that make you sad or angry. That only prolongs the negative emotions, possibly stretching the negative emotion into a negative mood.

Breathe Deeply for Inspiration

Among its other meanings, inspiration also indicates to breathe in. Deep breathing is central to managing your emotional state because it both determines and is determined by your emotions. Learning how to breathe fully hands you the reins to tame your alligator. The art of breathing gives you the ability to infuse your self with inspiration.

The breath is the bridge which unites the mind, the body and the spirit. All three of these areas are closely related to your emotional state through your constant awareness of your breath. When all is said and done, you calm down your 'gator (i.e., your emotions) by learning to control your body and your mind. Part of it is physical and part of it is mental. The best place to begin is by learning to focus your attention on your breathing – throughout the day. The emphasis on proper breathing is found throughout our history in the ways of most spiritual traditions – Hinduism, Zen, Buddhism, and Christianity.

When you "watch" your breathing over several weeks time, you will begin to notice a critical pattern. Each negative emotion adversely affects how you breathe.

Anger, for instance, is marked by shallow inhalation and forced, inflated exhalation.

Extreme sadness, on the other hand, is reflected by sporadic and shallow inhalation and minimal and fragile exhalation.

Fear is characterized by minimal breathing all the way around. Fear is marked by holding your breath so the inhalation and exhalation is nearly non-existent.

As you become more aware of these patterns, you recognize them more quickly, and remind yourself to breathe deeply. The mere act of breathing like a baby, into your belly, ratchets down the intensity of the negative emotion.

Deep breathing is one of the more powerful ways to reconnect your body, mind and spirit especially when situations get emotional. Anytime a strong negative emotion arises, it is wise to remove yourself from the situation (if possible). Find a quiet place where you will not be disturbed. And then try the following breathing exercise.

Deep Breathing Exercise

Find a quiet place where you will not be disturbed. This might be a bedroom, a bathroom or a quiet office. Sit comfortably in a chair or lying down on a bed or the floor. If you are sitting, your spine should be straight up and down but not quite rigid.

Once you are comfortable, loosen your pants and belt if necessary. Then, raise your shoulders by tensing your muscles in the neck, shoulders and back. Tense and relax your shoulders 3 times to release the tension. Then just allow your shoulders to hang loosely. Focus your attention on the weight of your shoulders.

Now close your mouth. Tuck your lightly into your chest. Close your eyes. Breathe slowly, deeply and completely into your abdomen, just short of any sense of uncomfortable pressure. As you inhale, pretend you are inflating your lungs like a balloon. Imagine a line just below your belly button. Breathe into this line so that your belly moves downward and slightly outward. If you place your hand on your stomach, you should be able to feel your stomach rise and fall (or go in and out if you are sitting) with each breath.

As you exhale, allow your belly to relax and return to its original position (back up and in). It's important when doing deep breathing to focus on breathing out all the old, stale air in your lungs. As you exhale, tighten the muscles in your abdomen. Pull the muscles in your stomach towards your back, the spine. This will help you expel all the old toxic air from your lungs. This is critical because most of us walk around all day holding carbon dioxide (poison!) in 4/5th of our lungs. Carbon dioxide is toxic and needs to be expelled from the body so you can replace it with vital oxygen. Simply doing this one exercise for three minutes per day will lead to tremendous benefits in your life. This exercise will allow you to experience what it was like to breathe back when you were a baby. I call it belly breathing where you breathe into your belly normally, naturally and fully.

As belly breathing become second nature to you, you will begin to apply it to your daily life – work, home, parenting, and sports. Your breath will synchronize with the demands of the task you face. Eventually, you will come to understand that your breath inspires your body, filling you with graceful and easy movements. Just remember, whenever your heart rate jumps, whenever you feel tense, angry or scared, take one minute to relax and breathe deeply. You will feel the change in your mood within seconds. Awareness of your breath is one of the most powerful ways to manage the energy of your emotions, the death-rolling alligator.

Breathing Visualization

Here's a powerful twist on the deep breathing exercise. Remember your brain is literal. It does not differentiate between what is "out there" and what goes on inside you (e.g., thoughts and feelings). Multiple brain scan studies have shown that the same areas in the brain activate whether you are looking at a baby or imagining a baby. This means that visualization, using your imagination, is an extremely powerful tool to help you manage your emotions and your life.

While doing your deep breathing, try this visualization exercise. Visualization is just a fancy way of saying use your imagination to envision something that helps calm you down and encourages positive emotions. For instance, while inhaling, picture a white light of serenity and calmness entering every cell of your body. As the white light enters your body, see it pushing the anger out of every pore of your skin. When exhaling, imagine your angry feelings, thoughts and tension leaving your body as a cloud of dark smoke.

The white light that you imagine inhaling can be anything you need at that moment: peace, relaxation, love, freedom from pain, healing, God's love, energy, or whatever else you want to substitute in.

The black smoke that you "exhale" can be anything that you need to expel from your body: pain, anger, fear, sadness, doubt, intrusive thoughts, tension, fatigue, and more. Experiment with your own needs and find what works best for you. These breathing and visualization skills are universal, will benefit all aspects of your life and can be used to counter any and all negative emotions. The trick is remembering to breathe when you are smack in the middle of an emotional hijacking.

Now I'll move on to shame.

Shame

Shame is the emotional pain that comes as a result of accepting the core belief that something is wrong with you. Shame makes you feel worth "less" than others. It is feeling badly for the kind of person that you believe yourself to be. When shame dominates your landscape of emotions, you live beneath a constant shadow. With shame, you are a prisoner of the past, imprisoned by current fears and incapable of facing the future with courage.

The feeling of shame is similar to what you feel like when you think of your mother angrily shaking her finger at you.

Your life will improve as soon as you are sincerely able to imagine what life will be when you are free from the emotional terrorism that is shame. Begin to dream of what your life should be, could be and will be now that you know you are eligible for all the joys life has to offer. You no longer have to disqualify yourself from happiness, material rewards and meaning just because you are you. You are worthy of everything great that life has to offer merely by virtue of the fact that you are a human being. As a human being you are entitled to respect, happiness and dignity. Let no one tell you differently.

Two Types of Shame

There are two types of shame: positive shame and negative shame. Negative shame is painful and overwhelming. It isolates you and causes you to turn against yourself. Negative shame lies to you by telling you that you are a bad person because of your shortcomings or failures. Negative shame tells you to take the blame when someone else trespasses across your personal boundaries. Negative shame makes you believe that taking steps towards a meaningful and happy life are hypocritical or deceitful. Negative shame occurs when you view your mistakes a true reflection of who you are. Destructive shame doesn't differentiate between a failed act and a failed person. Destructive shame is noticeable when you experience ongoing bouts of depression, you isolate yourself, you rely on substances to numb your pain, and when your public self is quite different from your private self.

Positive shame acts as a personal ethical warning system. Positive shame warns you of potentially dangerous or tempting situations. Positive shame keeps you out of situations which could potentially get you into serious trouble, such as marital infidelity, drinking and driving, violence, drug use, and theft. I like to think of positive shame as a "Spidey-sense" (like my childhood idol Spiderman) for situations that could possibly lead to irrevocable loss or major trouble down the road.

Physiological Cues of Shame

When you feel ashamed, your head and shoulders drop and blood rushes to the face and makes it appear redder. In addition to blushing, your posture constricts in terms of your physical space. In other words, when ashamed, you physically pull inward to make yourself feel and appear smaller.

Shame is the inner pain that comes from accepting the belief that something is innately wrong with us. Shame makes us feel worth less than others. This is distinctly different from guilt when we feel guilty for doing something wrong. Shame, on the other hand, is feeling guilty simply for being you.

Tips To Mitigate Shame

Shame begins with one of three sources: significant others, a shameful environment and/or a shameful event. Shame placed on you by significant others means that you were told or taught that there is something wrong with you. Shame due to a negative environment has to do with living in degrading circumstances that lessen your human dignity and/or situations that make you feel inferior to other people. A shameful event can negatively color the rest of your life by making you feel permanently marked in a negative manner.

Once you identify the sources of your shame, you will be able to find a wealth of resources that can help you with each one. A partial list of resources available to you includes yourself (your intelligence, emotional awareness, resiliency, courage and hope are the best resources), teachings to give you a new framework to view the world, groups to help you understand the shame and develop new skills, supportive individuals and your higher power.

Guilt

While shame is feeling distressed over who you are, guilt is feeling distress over what you have done. Guilt is based on your behavior, whereas shame is related to your entire being. Often, guilt and shame get intertwined into one big mess of emotions which causes great pain (emotional and physical), the desire to flee from yourself, and a feeling of being overwhelmed by your hidden burdens. True guilt results when you do something that is wrong or when you don't do something you know to be right.

Specifically, guilt follows on the heels of events such as infidelity, lying, cheating, stealing, and neglecting personal duties. Guilt usually involves your inner moral self. It follows transgressions of moral rules that govern behavior towards others. Often we attribute guilt to our lack of effort, whereas shame is attributed to a lack of ability.

When you feel guilty, you think you were in the wrong and that you shouldn't have done what you did or feel as you felt. It is frequently accompanied by a strong feeling of empathy, an awareness of others' feelings and a motivation to alleviate distress through action, confession and apology. There exists less self-consciousness and feelings of inferiority relative to embarrassment and shame. Upon feeling guilt, you feel like undoing what you have done and feel like punishing yourself. The end result of all this is typically the urge to apologize. The goal of guilt is to motivate you to make up for what you have done wrong and to ask forgiveness from yourself and the party you offended.

By labeling your guilt and shame and bringing them to the light of day, you can start to deal with both more effectively.

Example of Guilt: Julie was a 12-year-old gifted student who was distraught and depressed due to the death of her infant cousin. Julie's teacher referred her to me as she could not do anything in class but cry. When I spoke with her, she told me about the heart defect that had taken the life of her beloved cousin, a 6-month-old girl. Julie began to cry and shake with anger as she told me of the unfairness of the baby's death. She asked me why God would do such a terrible thing. This was the question that troubled the depths of her young soul. I had no answer. I said, "It seems like you are very angry with God because He took your cousin away." "That's right," she said. I asked her if she was comfortable being angry with God. "Oh, no! I feel terrible. I feel guilty. I can't be angry with God." I told Julie it was normal to be angry when someone you love dies. I also told her that it was okay to be angry with God since God is big enough to handle any emotion we send his way. After all, God made us and He made our emotions. He can handle our anger. He understands why we're angry. He forgives us for our anger and loves us no matter how we feel towards Him. Julie began to calm down. We continued to talk for a few minutes. She wiped the tears from her eyes, said "Thank you" and returned to class. The next day her mother called. "Are you the psychologist who spoke with my daughter yesterday?" "Yes, that's me," I replied. Julie's mother thanked me for speaking with her daughter. She said that Julie had been depressed and reclusive ever since the death. However, her mood had lightened since our talk. That is the power of guilt. It will eat you up.

Tips to Get Rid of Guilt

The solution to rid yourself of legitimate guilt is to:

a.) Identify your guilty feelings,

b.) Accept responsibility for the moral boundaries which you've violated,

c.) Confess the exact nature of your transgressions to yourself, another human being and to God, and

d.) Ask for forgiveness from yourself and others whom your
    actions negatively impacted.

Keep in mind that all of us have made mistakes. No one is perfect.
I've found that the burden of my guilt was eased in direct proportion to
the growth of my ability to forgive others their transgressions against me.
And as I learned to forgive others, I began to learn how to forgive myself.
Many times it is most difficult for us to forgive ourselves.

For more on this, please see the end of this chapter which provides
general tips on releasing negative emotions.

Genetic vs. Current Temperament

Let us return to temperament for a moment. I mentioned earlier that you have the power to positively influence your temperament. To explore this idea further, a critical distinction needs to be made. I consider there to be two different levels of temperament. There is your *genetically-predetermined temperament* and your *current temperament*. The genetically-predetermined temperament is the temperament with which you were born. It is primarily determined by your genes. However, genes only determine the range within which you can develop any particular aspect of your self. It is up to you to train your temperament to be as positive as your genetic range allows. *Your genetic temperament is not etched in stone. It can be influenced by you.* Genetic temperament is the long-term emotional style that is associated with your family tree and its respective gene pools. While rage is an emotion, a person with a chronically irritable disposition has an angry temperament.

Current temperament is differentiated from genetic temperament to make the point that your current temperament is NOT the same as your genetically determined temperament. Your happiness set point is amazingly malleable. You simply need to learn the tools to move yourself up the scale of life satisfaction.

My current temperament is calm, grateful and content. My genetically determined temperament is moody, irritable and anxious. It took me approximately 18-24 months to make this powerful change. This is a little distinction with huge implications.

As an example of the power of the genetic temperament, one study looked at individual's satisfaction with life between three groups – paraplegics, ordinary people and lottery winners. The study found the differences between the three groups in terms of their perceived sense of well-being were negligible at best.[37] This is particularly surprising given that the paraplegics, despite the trauma of losing a limb, started to feel positively only a few weeks after the accident that disabled them. Within one year, most of these individuals returned to their positive (or negative) outlook just as prior to their accident. The same pattern is seen in those who lose a loved one. They return to their genetic set point approximately one year after losing their loved one. In addition, there is almost no difference in daily moods between individuals who have modest annual incomes and those who are quite wealthy. In summary, there is little relationship between your life circumstances and your mood. We each have a set point for happiness that is genetically determined. That's the bad news. The good news is that you have the ability to move your set point towards greater overall happiness.

Rewriting Your Emotional Wiring

Don't keep running the rat race until you lose your mind. Learn to unwind instead!

Recent research on the brain mechanisms that underlie individual differences in emotional reactivity have provided strong evidence that *you have the ability to rewrite your emotional wiring.*[38],[39],[40] In 2003, Richard Davidson demonstrated that meditation training for employees of a fast-paced, high stress biotech company significantly decreased their anxiety, improved the functioning of their immune system, and improved their overall satisfaction with life.[41] Rather than being viewed as a fixed trait, temperament is now seen as a trait open to influence. Davidson taught the participants of his study one way to rewrite their emotional wiring – meditation.

In his book, *Learned Optimism*, Martin Seligman, a professor at the University of Pennsylvania, demonstrated that people can learn to be more realistically optimistic which results in less pessimism and more optimism. A greater degree of realistic optimism has a smorgasbord of health benefits which include a longer life span of up to 10 years, boosted immune system functioning, higher satisfaction with life, improved social relationships, and less depression.[42] Thus, both Davidson and Seligman have shown that our temperament is not permanently fixed. Rather our temperament is so subtle that most of us simply have not recognized its existence. What's more, we've assumed that temperament is etched in stone. It's not. You can change how you look at the world and realize enormous benefits in your home and work life.

Even short-term training (as little as 6 to 7 weeks) in how to regulate your emotions can produce significant effects on your day-to-day function.[43] What's more, the effects of these interventions are far-reaching and long-lived. Some studies have demonstrated that the positive effects of learning emotional regulation remain three years after the initial teachings.[44] I will discuss specific techniques in how to accomplish this later on in this book.

How to Wake Up to Emotional Awareness

Most of us are asleep at the emotional wheel. We are asleep and we don't even know that we're asleep. You need to wake up and begin to notice your feelings. Wake up to the realization that there are millions of ways to view the world. There is not just one reality. There are billions. In fact each of us have at least several ways of viewing reality depending upon our feelings, our temperament, our physical condition, our spiritual beliefs, our financial situation, our past experiences, and so on. And the way in which you view the world is your choice. Once you are emotionally aware, you can choose how to respond to the world. In choosing how to respond to the world, you will change your entire life.

There are many different layers to what we view as reality. Your perception of each of these layers is influenced by your internal state, external conditions and prior experiences. These layers are often influenced by things such as your physical state, spiritual awareness, religious affiliation, emotional awareness, intelligence, the geographic area in which you live, personality traits, race, gender, culture, age, experiences, social skills, mental stability, emotional stability and more.

The Breadth of Our Emotions

All emotions are essentially an impetus to act. Emotions are the evolutionary blueprint for handling life. The idea of emotions leading to action is most apparent in children. It is only in the adult world that we have divested thought from feeling and feeling from action. Fortunately, we now know several ways which, when practiced with some persistence and consistency, can lead to greater emotional management and more positive emotions.

Think Positive Thoughts

There are a number of proven ways in which you can increase the amount of positive affect in your life. One way to foster more positive emotions is to *think* so many positive thoughts that you leave no room for negative emotions. Positive *thoughts* lead to positive *emotions*. You can consciously create positive emotions by thinking about constructive emotions such as love, compassion and kindness. Merely focusing on the memory of an event in which someone performed a morally courageous act serves to lift us up emotionally. Jon Haidt, professor at University of Virginia, calls this emotion elevation and is currently at work trying to discern whether this is a new positive emotion.[45]

We know that positive thoughts lead to positive emotions due to a field of psychology known as cognitive behavioral therapy, or CBT.

The fathers of CBT, Aaron Beck and Albert Ellis, discovered that *what* you consciously think has a massive effect on *how* you feel.[46] While negative emotions arise largely due to circumstance, positive emotions can be cultivated by positive thoughts of joy, consideration and benevolence. The more time you spend contemplating concepts such as gentleness and love, the more you will increase the amount of positive emotional energy in your reservoir.

Become Aware of the Emotion in the Moment

One of your goals is to become aware of the bodily cues associated with each emotion more and more quickly until you can identify each emotion *in the split second that it occurs.* Take little steps in the direction of reducing the time it takes you to recognize when you are overtaken by an emotion.

For instance, fear is associated with blood flowing to the major skeletal muscles to prepare you for fleeing, anger with the

One way to feel happier is to think of getting a big hug from a loved one.

blood flowing to the hands to ready for fighting, and sadness with a drop in energy to help recover from a loss. In addition, every negative emotion is accompanied by an increase in heart rate. A jump in your heart rate is the biggest clue that you have just been hijacked by a negative emotion.

The more quickly you can recognize the physical cues, the faster you can recognize the emotion that is overcoming you. The faster you are aware of the onset of the emotion, the more rapidly you can take steps to interrupt the process and turn down the volume on your emotional responses or substitute positive emotions for your negative ones. Once you have accomplished that level of emotional mastery, you can focus on creating a more positive and pervasive temperament by changing your brain in meaningful and enduring ways. The first step is to become intimately familiar with how your body speaks the language of emotion to you.

Research done by Michael Bernet, Ph.D. has revealed three different types of people and how they typically interpret the bodily sensations attached to their own emotions.

The first type of individual is in touch with their body and their emotions. They demonstrate an automatic, integrated awareness of the subtle nuances of bodily cues that precede or exist simultaneously with a given emotion. They are called the Based on Body group or BB for short.

The second group, called the Looking to Logic group (LL), inserts logical reasoning between their emotions, the bodily sensations, and their response. The use of logic is an attempt to control their emotions or to avoid the potential discomfort of their emotions. This group is usually highly intellectual, analytical and relatively disconnected from their emotions.

The third group has a large disconnect between their emotions and the accompanying bodily cues. This third group, called the Emphasis on Evaluation group (EE), tends to dwell on negative ideas which often lead to self-doubt and anxiety. The EE group tries to understand what is happening in terms of ideals or expectations. The EE group uses the words "should" and "ought" frequently, expecting reality to conform to their ideal.

Amazingly, Dr. Bernet found that the BB group had better mental health, higher awareness of subtle bodily changes, more developed social skills, as well as greater contentment and creativity. The EE group was found to worry more, doubt themselves more and were less content. The LL group showed no relationship to mental health. However, the LL group did report being more socially reserved, and stressed the importance of intellect over social skills and emotional intelligence. What's more, the BB group was more likely to have sought out therapeutic experiences of

Learn to manage your worries. Ask yourself, "Will this matter a year from now?" If the answer is "No", which it is 99 times out of 100, then let the worry go!

all kinds. People who scored high on the LL scale were shown to rarely seek out any form of therapy.

The BB style (i.e. being in touch with one's feelings), is a useful predictor of social intelligence, emotional intelligence, physical health and well-being. Not surprisingly, those with the highest intelligence (top 2%) scored highest on LL and near the bottom on BB and EE. While those who picked up their questionnaires in a therapist's waiting room, scored highest on the EE scale. In other words, they were most likely to be unhappy, nervous or irritable and were looking for outside help and guidance with their emotions.

Our deepest fear is not that we are inadequate. Our deepest fear is that we are powerful beyond measure. It is our light, not our darkness, that most frightens us. We ask ourselves, who am I to be brilliant, gorgeous, talented and fabulous? Actually, who are you not to be? You are a child of God! Your playing small doesn't' serve the world. There's nothing enlightened about shrinking so that other people won't feel insecure around you. We were born to make manifest the glory of God that is within us. It's not just in some of us; it is in everyone. And as we let our own light shine, we unconsciously give other people permission to do the same. As we are liberated from our own fear, our presence automatically liberates others. - Nelson Mandela

---

Perhaps most importantly, the results indicate that the greatest improvement in overall well-being is attained through an integration of counseling with body and spiritual disciplines, or a holistic approach to health. These findings hold great promise for speeding the process towards happiness and meaning while lowering the cost. In addition, most psychotherapy could be easily improved by incorporating exercises that draw more attention to the correct identification of emotion via bodily sensations.

Emotional Options

With an awareness of your emotions as they occur, you have options available to you. You can simply note the existence of an unpleasant emotion. As your awareness grows, you will learn to recognize your emotions as they take place. Once you are able to recognize your emotions in real time, you can choose to hold onto the positive ones and let the negative ones go. With sufficient practice, you can change negative emotions to more positive ones. You can control your emotions to allow you to express them in a more constructive manner and in the time and place of your choosing. You will know when you have become an emotional genius when you are able to stay calm and centered in the face of someone who is angry with you.

How to Deal with Negative Emotions

The ultimate goal, as Aristotle stated thousands of years ago, is equanimity, or evenness of mind. To me, that includes being able to manage your thoughts and behaviors, as well as your emotions. As emotions underlie everything you do, it's imperative to find ways to defuse your negative emotions.

The first step in the process is to learn to speak the language of emotions - the bodily cues that alert you of the onset of an emotion. Once you become aware of your emotions as they occur, you can begin to master them. It is easier to allow negative emotions, such as anger and fear, to *flow through you* than to repress it or contain it. The emotion flows through you. Feelings are temporary. *The emotion is to be felt, recognized, honored and let go.*

Let me repeat this as it is very important. When you feel an emotion, such as happiness, anger or sadness, you want to listen to and honor the emotion. Once you have listened to each of your body's responses, understand them and label them. Accept any and all emotions as normal and natural. Then release them. Let 'em go. A simpler way of remembering how to master emotions is as follows:

Feel the bodily cues → *Become aware of the emotion* → *Honor the emotion* → *Let the emotion go* → *Breathe the negative stuff out and the positive in.*

Emotion is <u>not intended</u> to remain with you. An emotion is merely a call to action, an announcement of your needs and desires or those of others. Once it has done that, its purpose is fulfilled and that emotional energy must be allowed to return from whence it came. Nothing good happens when you hold on to negative emotional energy – anger, sadness, resentment, jealousy, and so on. The only person hurt when you remain angry at another is you. The only person damaged when you hold on to resentment is you. The only person weighed down when you retain sadness is you. Learn to let it go. Once you learn to honor and control your emotions, you will lead a much more peaceful and productive life.

Balance Between Negative and Positive Emotions

A balance between negative and positive emotions is essential for a mastery of life. Equally important is a balance between your thinking mind and your feeling mind. In this world, in this time, our thinking mind tends to be overly developed. Since the Age of Reason we have put great stock in intelligence and reason. This has tipped the scale in favor of the thinking mind. Our inner voice, the dialogue in our head, is verbal by nature. It talks to us and about us. This is largely the result of the thinking mind although its direction is often influenced by the emotional mind.

If you desire to restore your balance between thinking and feeling, spend some time each day quieting your thinking mind, the internal voice in your head. This can be done through meditation or any mindless activity such as strolling in the woods, chopping wood, singing, praying or fishing. The key is that you must lose your "self", your internal dialogue, in the activity. If thoughts intrude on your quiet mind, simply observe them, and let them pass through your mind. Do not get upset, frustrated or deterred. Thoughts will inevitably come across your mind. Honor them and let them go. You may also try chanting or repeating a single word, mantra or prayer to quiet your mind. Some proven words are "One", "Om", "Love" and "Peace". With practice, the thoughts come less often. Eventually, you can teach your rational mind to be peaceful and silent.

Equanimity as the Goal

Equanimity, evenness of mind and mood, may be the primary virtue needed for the development of interpersonal relationships. The idea of equanimity dates back to Aristotle. It is the ability to remain on an even emotional keel, neither swinging into highs nor dipping into lows. It does not mean detachment from emotion, but does indicate the ability to see, to observe one's emotions while they are happening and thus prevent being completely taken over by the emotion occurring at the moment. All emotions are held with equal honor. Through equanimity a refinement of our emotional life occurs.

Equanimity is tremendously important because through it we are able to develop a realistic understanding of our faults along with our strengths. For example, if you experience strong anger, equanimity makes it possible to be fully present in this anger without being taken over by it. You can step back and observe the anger without getting too caught up in it. While in an angry state, you can decide which type of anger you are experiencing and whether you should calm down or use your anger to enable a constructive solution.

Negative Emotions and Moods

Negative emotions cause us to be distrustful, retreat inward, and adopt a bunker mentality. Negative emotions lead us to a "man-all-battle-stations" mentality which usually results in a "lose-lose" situation. In a negative state of mind, you focus on what is wrong and then seek to eradicate it. This is in stark contrast to a positive state-of-mind which lifts people up into open-mindedness, creativity, generosity, and non-defensiveness.

Not all negative emotions are necessarily destructive, although many can be. Negative emotions narrow your focus and restrict the number of available actions and potential thoughts. Fear, for example, narrows your actions to three possibilities – fleeing, freezing or fighting.

Pick your Mood to Fit the Task

The idea is to pick your mood to suit your needs. If you need to think critically, such as studying for a test, dealing with social rejection, editing text, or doing taxes, you can effectively do so while sad, tense or anxious. However, if the task at hand requires creative thinking, generosity, or open-mindedness, you will be better off doing it in an environment that fosters positive emotions. Such an environment might include friends who are supportive and non-judgmental, a warm and sunny day, the sound of the ocean waves, the smell of a BBQ and upbeat music.

How to Foster Positive Emotions

Positive emotions signal that you are thriving and flourishing. Positive emotions also *create* flourishing! Positive emotions are worth cultivating. They are a means to achieving psychological growth and improved well-being over time. A positive mood leads to growth and personal development. These are the quintessential traits of a win-win situation. Positive emotions broaden your habitual modes of thinking, perceiving and acting which results in the building of greater physical, social, intellectual and emotional resources. This enables us to better deal with stressful situations down the line. Positive emotions are the key to filling your reservoir with positive energy.

Positive emotions have a host of health benefits for you. They help you to adapt to extremely distressful situations. They replenish resources that have been spent during stressful episodes. This is even seen at a cardiovascular level where cardiovascular recovery from negative emotions was speeded up by positive emotions.[47] The expression of positive emotions by a partner during the discussion of an upsetting film had a calming cardiovascular effect.[48] When looked at all together, positive emotions promote healthy body, mind and relationships in a number of ways.[49]

It is not merely that positive emotions are pleasant in their own right. It is that positive emotions cause much better interactions in the world. When you nurture positive emotions in your life, you build better relationships, create improved physical health, increase the amount and depth of love around you, and foster higher levels of accomplishment.

Positive Psychology

Martin Seligman is considered the father of positive psychology, a movement that began around 1998 when he was President of the American Psychological Association. Dr. Seligman is a distinguished professor at the University of Pennsylvania. Seligman has put forth a theory of happiness that essentially combines three traditional theories of happiness.

Three Kinds of Happiness

Seligman's theory holds that are three distinct kinds of happiness: the Pleasant Life, the Good Life, and the Meaningful Life.

The **Pleasant Life** is comprised of sensual pleasures, thoughts and feelings that take place in the present moment, such as vibrant sexual pleasure, massage, beautiful sunsets, pleasant scents, and exquisite meals. Pleasures of the senses are fleeting and cannot be sustained. While we know we can attain momentary happiness via sensual pleasures, it is not the best way to pursue a life of meaning and happiness due to its inherent unsustainability.

The **Engaged Life** is based on the relatively new theory of using your strengths rather than shoring up your weaknesses. The Engaged Life is defined as your degree of engagement in life, the extent to which you are aware of and use your strengths in your daily life. The more that you are engaged, the more happiness you have. Engagement has also been described as being in the "zone" or in the "flow."[50]

The **Meaningful Life** is based upon the spiritual or moral beliefs that you hold and the extent to which your actions are in keeping with your spiritual and/or moral values. The first two are subjective, the third is somewhat objective and hinges upon belonging to a community of people and serving something or some cause that is greater than your self, such as God.

Guide To Self has developed a set of 26 strengths, or values, based on a thorough review of the literature involving strengths and values that are found throughout the world. These values can be accessed at our website at http://www.guidetoself.com. To the extent that you are aware of your values and revel in them daily, you will increase the degree to which you are engaged in life and ultimately your level of happiness.

Building Emotional Intelligence

In general, mastery of your emotions consists of four parts: emotional self-awareness, emotional self-management, relationship management, and social awareness.[51] **Emotional awareness** is the ability to recognize your emotions as they occur and the impact that they have on your performance. It also entails a realistic optimism based on your past accomplishments. **Emotional self-management** consists of trustworthiness, self-discipline, and being calm under fire. It is primarily the capacity to keep negative emotions in check. **Social awareness** is the ability to sense and understand the emotional and political undercurrents of groups, whether they be your family or your work group. It also involves an awareness of other peoples' concerns and emotions. **Relationship management** exists when you can effectively give and take emotionally-laden information. When you can deal with difficult issues in a straightforward manner, then you can use your emotions to inspire and motivate others. The step of emotional awareness is listed first since low emotional awareness can bias your perceptions and block optimistic thoughts.

Emotional Intelligence

In this chapter, I will touch on the two internal parts of emotional intelligence, or emotional self-awareness and self-control. The best way to awaken your emotional intelligence is to be familiar with both of these areas which make up intrapersonal emotional intelligence, or the emotional skills within yourself.

Emotional Self-Awareness

Emotional self-awareness is the ability to recognize your own emotions and the impact that they have on your performance. Peter Salovey, a psychologist from Yale, describes emotional self-awareness as knowing one's emotions, as recognizing an emotion *as it takes place*.[52] This second-by-second awareness is the cornerstone of emotional intelligence. The ability to be aware of emotions from moment to moment throughout the day is critical to psychological insight, growth and self-understanding. If you cannot notice your feelings as they happen, you are left to their mercy. When you have an awareness of your feelings, in the moment, you are more confident in your decision-making because you know how you feel about your different options.

Perhaps the best way to illustrate this is with a story.

My wife and I are parents of four children – two daughters and two sons. My oldest daughter is eleven, my first son is nine, my youngest son is six and my baby girl is 6 months. My children are lifelong lessons in emotional awareness and self-control. They are all great kids. Yet, there is no greater challenge than to parent well.

Awhile back, my oldest son felt ashamed when he cried. He felt that boys aren't "supposed to cry." I told him that crying was fine. Everyone cries – boys and girls. He asked me if I cry. I told him I did. He asked if he could see me when I was crying. I told him that I would do my best although I had my doubts because I hadn't cried a tear in years due to my own struggle with emotional repression.

Shortly after our conversation, I was in a great deal of pain due to sciatica. Sciatica is a condition where a particular nerve is pinched, leading to shooting pain in the low back and one leg. This pain is neural pain and thus cannot be diminished by medication, ice or heat. I was scheduled to go in for an epidural (an injection of cortico-steroids in the spine) to alleviate the swelling the next day. That night, I was lying in my bed on several ice packs to dull the pain. The pain was so debilitating that I couldn't even sit up to watch television. Frustrated and dejected, I began to cry silently. My wife sat by my side and watched with quiet compassion, knowing there was nothing she could do to help me out.

In the midst of feeling sorry for myself, I remembered my commitment to my son to share my tears with him. It was at that moment that I realized that I could simultaneously feel an emotion and observe it with my rational mind.

As my wife and I had just put the children to bed, I asked my wife to get my son out of his bed so he could see me cry. My wife went in to the room where my two oldest children slept and told them that that I was crying. They flew into my bedroom to witness my tears. Upon seeing my tears, my son was immediately filled with compassion and caring for my plight. Now, he feels far less shame when he cries. I don't know if he is free of shame, but it was a big step in the right direction.

Did you ever see your father cry? I never did. Were you given permission to express your feelings? If we are to act as role models for our children, friends, and coworkers, we must be willing to share our emotions openly to the extent that they are not harmful to others. This is especially critical for men and boys who have not been given permission in the past to express emotions freely. Think of it as a shift in generational paradigm. Earlier generations were taught not to show emotions. We now know that emotions exist for a purpose. Those who are skilled in recognizing, honoring and controlling their emotions are well on their way to success in their life. Teach yourself and those around you how to recognize and manage their emotions and everyone will benefit.

Knowing your emotions, or emotional self-awareness, is the foundation of emotional intelligence and the basis for positive emotional energy. You need to be aware of your emotions as they occur if you want to maximize your potential and increase your chance at a happy and successful life. *If you are not aware of your emotions, then your emotions are in control of you.* The more you are aware of your feelings, the more that you are able to steer your own life.

Emotional self-awareness allows you to be confident about critical choices such as who to marry, where to live, whether to have babies and how to raise your children. Emotional self-awareness is the realization that your emotions have a huge impact on your performance – in the workplace, at home, within yourself, and in all your relationships, including your relationship with God.

Emotional Self-Management

The next area of emotional intelligence is emotional self-management, which is the ability to remain calm under fire. It is the capacity to retain an even mood while people around you are getting increasingly angry, sad or anxious. This is the ability to appropriately deal with your feelings. Emotional self-awareness is a necessary precursor for emotional self-management. Without self-awareness, there can be little self-management. People who are low in this area are easily overwhelmed by the inevitable ups and downs of life. Those that excel in this area have realized the power of positive emotional energy and thus have an inner resiliency that enables them to bounce back quickly from negative emotions. Individuals who are advanced in this area can rebound from significant negative emotions in a matter of seconds.

The Power of Resiliency

Another critical part of emotional self-management is resiliency, the ability to bounce back quickly from difficulties, setbacks, and unexpected negative events. Barbara Fredrickson at the University of Michigan recently demonstrated that resilient people have a greater reservoir of positive emotional energy.[53] It has also been shown that more of us are naturally resilient than was previously thought. We used to think that only a handful of people had this tremendous psychological resiliency which allowed them to bounce back from trauma and loss. Recent findings have shown that more than half of us (46% to 78%) already are capable of authentic resilience in the face of loss.[54] This is an incredibly powerful jump in the knowledge base of humankind. For years, we have known that resiliency is a key trait in determining which children would emerge unscathed from terrible circumstances such as abuse, neglect, trauma, low socioeconomic conditions and more. However, we didn't know much at all about what exactly resiliency was.

In 2000, Fredrickson demonstrated that positive emotions provide the foundation for greater resiliency. This means that the cultivation of positive emotions help people cope with stressful and traumatic events. Just as resilient metals bend but don't break, resilient people will bend with life's negative events, but they never give up. They bounce back. They don't break.

On top of this, it was found that resilient people show a faster cardiovascular recovery after experiencing an extremely intense negative emotion. This is critical to understand. Every time you are hijacked by a negative emotion, your heart rate rises, your blood flow is diverted from where it is needed, and your brain narrows its focus and becomes less creative and open-minded. The way to break out this cycle is to breathe deeply and focus on slowing your heart rate. The more quickly you can return your heart rate to normal, the more quickly you regain full control of your body and your mind.

It is thought that a deep reservoir of positive emotion facilitates a quick cardiovascular recovery which is closely related to resiliency. Fredrickson found that resilient individuals respond differently than non-resilient people to stressful events. Even when stressed by an anxiety-provoking task, such as giving an unprepared speech in front of a crowd, resilient individuals reported the same amount of high anxiety as others, yet they simultaneously experienced a much higher degree of happiness and genuine interest in the task. This demonstrates another fundamental belief that must be learned for you to operate at your potential. *You have the ability to feel more than one emotion at the same moment in time.* This simple statement has powerful ramifications.

For instance, my wife (who doesn't get upset with me *too* often) was upset with me recently. At the time, my reservoir was full of positive emotional energy. I knew that she was exhausted and frayed. Thus, her reservoir was empty at best, and filled with negative energy at worst. She began raising her voice to me. I was aware that she needed to vent and nothing I could say or do was going to change that.

At that moment an amazing thing happened. *My emotional brain split into two separate parts both of which I could control and retain awareness.* With one part (about 40% of my consciousness), I could listen to what she was saying and respond with appropriate words and emotions. With the other part, (about 60%) I could remind myself of a number of things to stay calm and centered. Let me give you an idea of what goes through my head during such an emotional outburst directed at me. First, I reminded myself that my wife was tired and had been working very, very hard. Second, I reminded myself that this was not a result of my action or inaction. Third, I reminded myself to breathe deeply in the midst of the emotional thunderstorm. Fourth, I told myself that she was merely expressing some negative emotion and I know that emotion eventually passes. Finally, there is a line in a song called 'Gone for Good' by The Shins that I like to use. The line states, "You want to fight for this love, but, Baby, you cannot wrestle a dove." I kept repeating the line "You can't wrestle a dove" to myself as a reminder that you cannot fight someone who refuses to fight back. You cannot meet anger with anger if you want to defuse a situation. Anger requires anger to combust. Anger cannot grow without more anger to fuel it.

Growing Emotional Self-Awareness and Self-Management

It is my belief that there are a series of developmental steps that we take in learning to be aware of our emotions. These developmental steps have implications in terms of whether we are in control of our emotions or they are in control of us.

1. No awareness of emotions.
    a. Emotions control you.
    b. Individual reacts according to current emotion.

2. Beginning awareness.
    a. Attempt to 'turn off' emotions or shut them down
    b. No emotional management.

3. Awareness of basic emotions.
    a. Little management of emotions. Many emotions last for weeks.
    b. Basic emotions: Sadness, anger, contempt, happiness, disgust, guilt, fear, surprise

4. Awareness of complex emotions.
   a. Awareness occurs hours or days after emotion oc-
      curs.
   b. Some emotional management. Emotions last for
      hours or days.
   c. Examples of complex emotions: Resentment, re-
      gret, love, gratitude, guilt, shame, maliciousness,
      embarrassment

5. Quicker awareness of complex emotions
   a. Awareness takes place seconds or minutes after
      emotion occurs.
   b. Increasing emotional management.

6. Awareness of basic emotions *as they occur.*
   a. Managing basic emotions in the moment.

7. Awareness of complex emotions as they occur.
   a. Manage complex emotions in the moment.

8. Ability to split emotional awareness
   a. Awareness is split between managing reality and
      managing emotions as they occur.
   b. Individual manages own emotions. Emotional
      self-management.

The goal of this whole process is the ability to recognize and manage
your emotions *in the moment.* Once you have developed this ability you
will have a number of options available to you. In this way, you can deal
with negative, destructive emotions as they arise. You will be able to think
clearly and calmly to brainstorm options, evaluate your possible courses of
action and pick the best possible behaviors for all involved.

Example: To give you an idea how this unfolds, let's look at the
emotional development of Jack. As an infant, Jack was not allowed by
his parents to voice negative emotions (e.g., anger, anxiety and sadness).
When he became angry and cried, he was yelled at by his parents. It was
the classic case of meeting anger with anger in which everyone loses. Jack's
parents were exhausted and overwhelmed and screamed at him to be quiet
when he cried. The more they yelled at him, the more he cried. As a result,

over time, Jack understood that there are certain emotions that could not be shared so he tried to shut them off. This created great anxiety in Jack. It also made it much harder for Jack to trust adults. While this is not a healthy way to learn to manage emotions, it has been an all too common tale for many. And, as we know, relationships in infancy set the foundation for later relationships.

During preschool, Jack learned to talk about and recognize his basic emotions, such as happiness and sadness, despite his early difficulties. With the help of a teacher, he began to understand that emotions are important signals that come from inside the body or from outside him. These signals gave Jack important information about his own needs and those of others around him. He began to put words together with certain emotions – scared, happy, safe and mad.

Over the next few years, Jack became aware of more complex emotions such as disappointment and pride. By the time he was twelve, he had learned even more involved emotions like embarrassment, humiliation, rejection, forgiveness and maliciousness.

Typically, the recognition of his own complex emotions came many days after he actually experienced the emotion. It was only upon looking back at an event that he could say, "Oh, when I tripped in the gym, it made me embarrassed." With age and experience, Jack gradually whittled down the amount of time it took between feeling the emotion and recognizing it. He eventually got quite good at identifying his emotions and by the age of 15, he could recognize an emotion as it came upon him. For instance, when someone teased him in high school one time, he realized that he was beginning to get angry due to the humiliation he was experiencing. He took a deep breath to help him control his anger and asked the other student, "Are you feeling malicious? Are you having a rough day today?" This was a very different experience for the other student. It confused him enough so that he stopped teasing Jack.

As an adult, Jack made another huge jump in his development, realizing that he could split his attention so he could simultaneously attend to what someone else was saying to him, focus on his breathing, and hold a calming image in his mind. This held true even when another person became upset with him.

This story illustrates the fact that no matter what our upbringing, we always retain the power to relearn the way in which we recognize and process emotions. The human brain is never done growing, learning or creating new connections. It is always changing due to our inner and outer experiences.

Identify Emotions As They Occur

As emotions are intertwined with every thought, perception and action you have, you must be able to accurately identify which emotion you are feeling *as you are experiencing it.* This takes practice. When you feel an emotion coming on, ask yourself, "What do I notice happening within my body?" and "What happened right before this emotion to possibly trigger it?" Emotions are incredibly important to our continued survival. Emotions help keep us on the right path by providing guide rails for our thoughts. Emotions set the parameters for our decisions. They steer us in certain directions. For example, sadness keeps us close to home during trying times. Anxiety readies us for action. And all emotions can provide us with valuable tips regarding our relationships with other people.

To further our discussion of emotions, it is important now to draw a distinction between the rational mind and the emotional brain.

Rational and Emotional Minds

One of the most important things to discover is that each one of us has a thinking, or rational, mind and a feeling, or emotional, mind. We used to think that we only had a rational mind. How's that for irony? The thinking mind only discovered itself.

Rational Mind

The thinking mind, the alligator wrestler, is the means that we usually use to understand the world – more aware, more thoughtful, and able to consider and reflect upon things outside of you, such as your friends and the forest, and upon things inside of you, such as thoughts and feelings. For instance I can reflect on the thought that I had earlier this morning that I should take a shower.

Emotional Mind

Alongside the thinking mind is another means of knowing – our emotional mind, the alligator. Your emotional mind is irrational, impulsive, creative and intense. Most times, your thinking mind is in charge of your mind and body. However, the more intense the feeling you are experiencing, the more prevalent the emotional mind becomes and the more useless your thinking mind is. Your brain is wired to make you an emotional being. You experience the emotional response to an event before it even reaches your rational mind. That is why sometimes you are overcome by your emotions. When the emotion is strong enough, your emotional mind temporarily takes over control of your mind and body in order to keep you safe. The emotional mind errs on the side of caution, of keeping your body safe. Before you are even conscious of it, your emotional mind picks up two to three important elements from your immediate surroundings, and decides whether or not there is a threat present. If a threat is determined to exist, or if there is a good probability that it exists, then the emotional mind takes over and prepares your body to fight or run away.

When your emotional mind takes over in such an emergency, real or perceived, it's known as an emotional hijacking. An emotional hijacking is impulsive, quick, strong, and raw.

Normally, part of your rational mind is always working to prevent emotional takeovers. This allows you to think about your emotions *before* you act on them. This enables us to respond to our emotions more appropriately. This typically takes slightly more time than an emotional hijacking, but it allows us to consider a number of different responses and usually results in a more thoughtful course of action. These responses include whether to attack or run, and also whether to persuade, cajole, beg, plead, charm, seek sympathy, instill guilt, act brave, or to be thoughtful. The responses include any and all of the possible actions that might result from the entire spectrum of emotions.

The Need for Emotion in Rational Thought

The fascinating piece of the puzzle is that we all need a balance between our thinking and feeling minds in order to lead successful and happy lives. Amazingly, the rational and the emotional mind *need each other* to function at their highest level. This means that you need your emotions to think straight!

I'll tell you a story to show you what I mean. I have an old friend who is one of the smartest guys I've ever met. He could recite word for word anything he had heard or read in his life. He could solve problems in school that no one else, not even our teacher, could solve. He devoured books by the boxful. He read everything he got his hands on. He used to tell me random facts he recalled from his parents' set of encyclopedias he read when he was only seven years old. Yet, he was unable to control himself and his ego. He was impulsive which means that he acted *before* he thought about the possible consequences of his actions. He was disruptive and troublesome in class. So here is this incredibly smart person with terribly flawed decision-making skills and poor emotional control. As he grew older, he made awful choices in his life. He wound up alone and unsuccessful. Some would argue that he could not access his emotional learning.[55] Your emotional learning is where you store your general likes and dislikes. Without a storehouse of prior emotional experiences to compare to present events, everything appears neutral -- neither appealing nor unappealing. This means that feelings are essential to thought.

Emotions steer us in the best direction where logic can be put to its best use. Without emotions, we'd be overwhelmed by the dazzling array of choices we need to make every minute of every day. Our emotional learning helps us sift through these options and pulls out the best ones to be analyzed by our thinking brain. In this way, emotions work as an equal partner with logical thought. The better these two partners work together, the higher your intelligence *and* your emotional intelligence.

Fostering Emotional Mastery

One of the most critical skills we learn as youngsters is the ability to soothe ourselves when we are upset. This means calming ourselves when we are irritated, angry, scared, anxious, sad, or depressed.

People who fail to learn this skill are forever fighting off chronic anxiety, sadness or irritability.

People who learn to manage their emotions persevere to overcome life's setbacks. They are resilient and rebound from disappointments more quickly. They have a positive, optimistic outlook on life.

The primary way to manage emotion is to acknowledge the emotion and then visualize it leaving your body. Picture the negative emotion leaving while breathing deeply into your abdomen and exhaling all of the old, stale air out of your lungs. Breathe deeply and continue this visualization exercise for 3 minutes. A mere three minutes of this can rid you of any emotion with sufficient practice.

Another way to gain a greater mastery of emotions is to get to know their patterns or tendencies and then anticipate when and where they will strike. What are the triggers that spark your negative emotions? Is it criticism from a loved one? Is it feeling overwhelmed at work? Is it fear of speaking in front of others? Is it fear of failing? You'll need to know what sets your anger off, what sets your fear off, and so on. This way you will be prepared for most situations. Prior to going into tense situations, breathe deeply for 3 minutes. Remind yourself to breathe while in the tense situation.

Emotions accompany every thought, perception and action you have, so you must be able to accurately identify which emotion you are feeling *as you are* experiencing it. This takes practice, awareness and intention. You must decide that you are going to become aware of your emotions. Pay attention to them all day long. When you feel an emotion coming on, ask yourself, "What do I notice happening within my body?" and "What happened right before this emotion to possibly trigger it?"

With most of my clients, it works best to teach them how to let go of their negative emotions which they've usually stuffed down for years.

Steps to Release Negative Emotions

Here are the steps to release your negative emotions and their destructive tendencies:

1.) Become Aware of the Negative Emotion
2.) Label Negative Emotion
3.) Ask Your Heart for Best Response
4.) Breathe Negative Emotion Out, Antidote In

Let me explain in more detail each of the above.

1.) Become Aware of the Negative Emotion

If you are immediately aware of the changing feelings in your body, *and you* interpret them correctly, *and you* respond to them properly, it is likely that you will do what is best for you. This means that you will respond in an optimal manner. On the other hand, if we suppress our emotions or incorrectly identify them or take too long time figuring out an appropriate response, we'll build up a mish-mash of misperceptions leading to inappropriate actions. Such misperceptions, misinterpreted emotions, and the ensuing negative interpretations of reality threaten to create an infinite downward spiral, building in negative energy and momentum. These downward spirals inevitably result in a totally inappropriate response to the initial situation.

Thus, you need to become more aware of your emotions *as they occur*. Take a *time out* when you realize your emotions are escalating. Stop everything. Life is a series of moments. Imagine the situation slowing down like the frames of movie. The movie gets slower and slower until it finally stops. At this point, you can become aware of your emotion. You can choose to focus on one of these moments with intention and awareness. This skill takes practice. Over time you will improve at slowing down emotionally charged situations so you can know when you are getting upset and take steps to intervene.

When my clients initially come to me, they usually need practice at recognizing their emotions in the moment. Often, they are able to recognize their emotions in hindsight. However, the goal is to be able to identify your emotions instantly, as they take place. Once you can identify your negative emotions in the moment, you will be better equipped to act upon it, and release it immediately. In this manner, your negative emotions lose all power over you.

2.) Label Your Negative Emotion in the Moment

Learn to immediately and correctly label your emotions. This step is critical. As soon as you recognize that your emotions are rising, stop what you are doing and take a time out. This step takes some practice as many of us have become so numb to our emotional state. Many of us are not even aware of negative emotion even as they eat away at us. Learn to identify your emotions in the moment.

Slow down, get quiet and ask your heart for an answer. Your heart has over 40,000 brain cells, or neurons, of its own!

3.) Ask Your Heart for the Best Response

Ask your heart, "What is the best way to respond to this situation?" Sometimes negative emotions, such as fear and anxiety, arise to warn us of impending danger. However, sometimes our emotions lie to us and make our body believe we are in a life-threatening situation when in truth there is no imminent physical danger (e.g., speaking in front of a crowd). Your job is to become better at discriminating between those emotions which require a subsequent action to mitigate the situation and those emotions that are deceiving you and simply need to be released.

Remind yourself to slow down and r-e-l-a-x!

Quiet your rational, thinking mind and listen to your heart and your feelings. Focus your awareness on your heart and listen. Often, I hear these heartfelt responses in the back of my head, whereas I experience most of my usual, rational thoughts towards the front of my head.

4.) Breathe Negative Emotion Out and Antidote In

Consciously, let the negative emotions go. For example, when you begin to get angry, tell yourself, "I'm feeling angry. That's alright. I'm going to let my anger go now." And breathe deeply into your abdomen. Breathe in for a count of 4 seconds, hold your breath for 1-2 seconds and breathe out for 6 seconds. Repeat this breathing cycle for a minimum of 3 minutes. You will find that this breathing pattern alone will help you to release negative emotions. It is designed to relax the body, reduce your heart rate and to bring your body to a peaceful state.

Remember an uplifting, positive feeling you have had in your life. Think of the sights, the smells, the sounds, the feel, and the taste of the moment that produced that feeling. Relive the moment and the positive feeling.

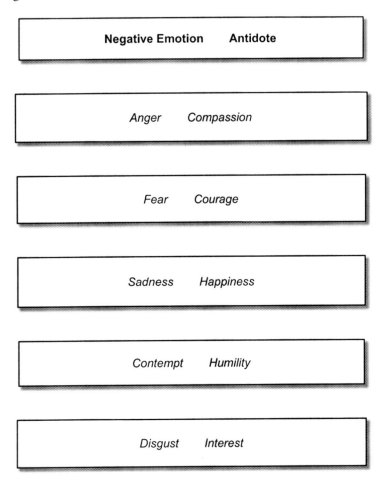

Negative Emotion	Antidote
Anger	*Compassion*
Fear	*Courage*
Sadness	*Happiness*
Contempt	*Humility*
Disgust	*Interest*

While breathing, envision negative emotional energy leaving your body as thick, black smoke and positive emotional energy rushing into your body as radiant white light.

Watch Your Thoughts

Realize that *your thoughts and feelings can lie to you.* Your thoughts and your feelings do not always tell you the truth. And in most situations involving a negative emotion, thoughts and feelings lie to you... frequently.

Your thoughts and feelings lie to you!
You MUST be aware of the lies
so you can challenge them!
Never, never, never give up.

Reframing the situation in a more positive, gracious light works well to defuse the sadness cycle. This means that you need to give others the benefit of the doubt. Pretend that they are acting in your best interests or that they have a valid reason for acting as they have. For example, your close friend, who calls you every year on your birthday, forgets to call on your birthday this year. You can choose to interpret it as a personal slight and get sad about it. Or you could reframe the situation such that you assume your friend must have had something very important going on to have missed your birthday call.

Five Areas That Influence Management of Emotional Triggers

Even masters of emotions lose control over their feelings at times. There are a number of situations where you need to be on guard because you are more likely to be emotionally hijacked. Emotions always have the power to seize control of your brain and body, even if you are consciously and cognitively aware that you are safe. If your emotional mind decides you are in danger, your body will react to keep you safe. In other words, your knowledge doesn't override the primal strength of emotions. Your brain is constantly making evaluations of what is safe, what is dangerous, what makes you angry and what makes you sad. These are called autoappraisals by Paul Ekman.

Emotions are more likely to occur when they are close to certain innate affective themes (e.g., a person threatening your family will trigger anger in you) or when they are close to an emotional trigger you've learned.

The scary part is that emotions can deprive you of every last piece of knowledge that you have learned throughout your lifetime. They are that powerful. When you are in the grip of a strong emotion, such as rage, your emotional mind takes over completely, depriving you of knowledge that you would have if you were not so angry. What's more, when you are in the grip of rage, you interpret the world through a rage-colored lens. You attend to things that confirm your rage and ignore those pieces of information that do not. It goes back to the idea that you find that for which you look. If you are angry, you automatically look for things to support your anger. If you are afraid, you seek out things to justify and extend your fear. You don't look to challenge your emotions. You seek to confirm them.

This is useful in situations where our safety is threatened. However, it can be dangerous in situations where you think your safety is in jeopardy when, in fact, you are safe. The same system that guides your attention and focus also distorts your perception of reality, disables your ability to take in new data and to access your existing knowledge.

Let's look at the example of Troy. Troy is an adult male who was verbally abused as a child by his father. Between the ages of 1 to 12, Troy's father would insult Troy in a voice laced with contempt and disgust. Nothing Troy did was ever good enough for his father. During Troy's little league games, his father would belittle his efforts and highlight his errors. At home, Troy was mocked, mimicked and teased. His father taunted him with dark sarcasm mercilessly. Within a short period of time, most likely within the first four to five years of his life, Troy developed an emotional script around older, more powerful men teasing him, even when it was not meant in a mean-spirited manner. This script was recorded in Troy's emotional database in his mind. Whenever his father teased him, Troy's anger would flash brightly, much to his father's delight. His dad would respond by teasing troy about his anger.

Fast forward, twenty years later, Troy is 32 years old and still reacts with rapid anger to the slightest sign of taunting, from anyone. Troy doesn't physically assault people who insult him, but his life would be much better if he didn't have the urge to slug everyone who teased him.

There are five areas that affect how effectively Troy can manage the intensity, power and length of his emotional reaction. The first idea to be aware of is *how close the current situation is to his existing emotional trigger.* He knows that teasing makes him overly angry. He knows that being teased by an older man is doubly difficult for him. The closer the current circumstances are to his original script, the harder it will be for Troy to manage his emotional reaction. Taunting from a woman will be easier to deal with than taunting from a man. Teasing from a younger person is easier to manage than from an older person. An older, male authority figure will be the hardest situation of all to manage. And this may be a problem if Troy encounters a policeman with a sarcastic attitude. So it's easier to manage the emotional trigger the further away you are from the existing emotional script.

Second, the *earlier in a person's life that the emotional script developed, the harder it will be to manage the trigger.* This is due to the fact that the younger you are, the less you have in terms of tools to deal with emotions. So you will have a stronger emotional reaction linked to the trigger from those events that took place early on in your life compared with those that happened later. Mounting evidence from neuropsychology and developmental psychology is demonstrating the importance of childhood experience in the development of the personality and your emotional landscape.

Third, *the more intense the emotions were* when the triggered was learned, the harder it will be to mitigate the trigger. In Troy's case, the feelings of shame, worthlessness and humiliation were strong initially. So it will be more difficult to weaken the impact when he gets teased as an adult. On the other hand, if his father's teasing led to mild emotion in Troy, then it would be easier to weaken the impact of the emotional trigger.

Fourth, the *frequency of the episodes* that initially created the emotional trigger has an impact. The more frequent the episode of intense emotions within a short period of time, the harder it is to defuse the emotional trigger. In Troy's situation, his father teased him daily. The episodes took place frequently and thus this emotional trigger is more difficult to manage.

Fifth, your *style of affect* plays a large role in how well you can diffuse an emotional trigger. Individuals vary in the intensity of their emotions, how rapidly emotions arise, how long the emotion stays, and how long it takes to recover from the emotion. If you are hit hard and fast by your emotions, then research shows that you will have a harder time defusing your triggers.

So, how do you go about defusing your emotional triggers? The first step is *awareness.* You must realize what your triggers are. What is it that sparks your anger? Who triggers your anxiety? Using the daily emotion journal, figure out what it is that makes you angry. You may not be aware what it is that sparks your anger. Remember that anger overtakes you in less than a third of a second. Awareness. Awareness. Awareness. If you want to tame the 'gator, you must become aware of the physical sensations that go hand in hand with anger, sadness and fear. If you can't figure out the triggers by yourself, a coach or counselor may be helpful in identifying them with you.

Once you are aware of the trigger, reframe the situation. What are the motives of the person who is making you angry? Are they intentionally making you angry? Is there another possible explanation? Are you taking things too personally? Come up with as many possible explanations for the scenario that you can. Learn to re-interpret situations more quickly. These steps will be discussed in more detail later in this chapter.

The great news is that we can develop and strengthen our emotional skills if we try. While our intelligence remains pretty much the same over time, our emotional skills grow with practice, just like muscles grow with strength training. Each of these areas is as it is within us because of our habits. Our habits and our routines have dictated to what extent our emotional skills have been developed. Most of us haven't really been aware of nor focused on improving our awareness of our feelings. The first step is to become aware of what you are feeling.

You can strengthen your emotional self-awareness by creating a well-traveled path between your emotional mind and your thinking mind. The more you think about what you are feeling and why you are feeling a certain way, the stronger the pathway becomes between your thinking mind and your feeling mind. Dealing effectively with emotions, especially intense ones like anger and fear, is essential to building friendships. When you react to your anger in a more productive way than normal, you actually are building new pathways in your brain that connect emotional experiences with reason.

This means that if you usually yell at your friends when you are angry with them, you must learn to choose another reaction, such as telling them why you are angry in a calm voice. *To get this reaction to become permanent, you must practice it many times before your urge to yell is replaced.*

Positive Emotions Are the Goal

The ultimate goal is to have three times as much positive emotion as negative emotion in your life. This is the cut off point for a thriving life as set by Barbara Fredrickson at University of North Carolina, Chapel Hill. Positive emotional energy has been associated with decreased anger, reduced depression, less sadness, better sleep, minimized stress and anxiety and greater physical energy.[56] Positive emotional energy has been associated with increased serenity, peacefulness and compassion for others. When you are filled with positive emotional energy, you believe in the inherent worth of your self. You are calmer and less likely to fly into anger when your emotional tank is full of positive energy. You can remain peaceful based on your inner state, regardless of external circumstances. And perhaps, most importantly, you can show compassion to others.

Stick with it. Emotional mastery takes time and practice.

A great deal of misunderstanding and irritation can be avoided if we have a full emotional gas tank. In other words, when we have a full reservoir of positive emotional energy, then we are more likely to support and love those around us.

Emotional Awareness Exercises

This section includes exercises, reminders, encouragements, and a sample daily chart to record your emotions and the factors which contribute to them. Keeping a daily emotion journal is a tremendously powerful tool for increasing your emotional intelligence.

Understand Your Triggers

To counter negative emotions, you will need to understand what sets you off. The first step to emotional mastery is to know what your triggers are. If you have not already, become aware of your emotional triggers, those situations or people that set you off. It is a good idea to keep a record of your emotions in your journal. Should you choose to do so, note down the following columns: Date, Emotion felt, intensity of emotion on a 1 (mild) through 10 (severe) scale, bodily signs (such as increased heart rate, furrowed brow, raised voice, perspiration, etc.), preceding events, events during and following emotion, your response, grade for your response on a 1 (poor) through 10 (excellent) scale, remember to breathe (yes or no), and the way in which you released your negative emotion.

The second step is to understand that your negative emotions are bad for you. Anger, fear, sadness and disappointment are harmful to your body on several levels when you hold onto them. Negative emotions can reduce the blood supply to your heart.[57] On top of that, negative emotions cause the body to respond by releasing adrenaline, noradrenaline and cortisol into the bloodstream. All of these hormones are helpful in small amounts. However, these hormones are damaging to your body when the levels get too high or remain for too long. Anger, sadness and fear damage your body if you hold on to them for long periods of time. Learn to let them go.

Adrenaline increases your heart rate and blood pressure, makes your breathing more shallow and rapid, prepares you for confrontation and tightens your muscles. When you are suffering from chronic stress and your body is producing high levels of cortisol over time, your immune system functioning declines, you lose bone and muscle mass more quickly, your fat accumulates more rapidly and your memory and learning are impaired. [58,59,60,61] The daily accumulation of little stressors does the majority of the damage by taking a constant toll on your body. Normally, you would rest to allow your body to recover from a stressful event. However, chronic stress creates a situation where you cannot rest enough to allow your body to fully recover. You put up with stress and its adverse consequences, but you don't have to. Now you have an alternative. Learn to change your perceptions.

Practice Catching Others Doing Good

You have been trained since your childhood to be on the look out for children, coworkers and friends doing bad things – lying, cheating, fighting, and tattling. This exercise involves actively seeking out the good in others and it takes some practice. I have three children, so I like to think of it as catching them doing something good.

For instance, the other day, my wife was driving our three children home from a birthday party. My daughter who is ten was sitting in the back seat of the Suburban with my son, Mason, who is eight. Mason had a bag of candy from the party which he was busily eating. Well, he began choking on a piece of hard candy, really choking, where he couldn't speak or breathe at all. My wife noticed he was choking and began to change lanes so she could stop on the shoulder of the freeway. In the meantime, rather than panicking, my daughter began slapping him hard on the back to dislodge the candy. And before my wife could stop the car, Bridget dislodged the candy from Mason's throat with her quick-thinking.

Now when I heard that story, I jumped on the chance to make Bridget into a 'hero'. I thanked her for saving Mason's life and told her that she was a life-saver. I complimented her on keeping her cool under difficult circumstances. She tried to pass it off as nothing but I drew her attention to the fact that if she HAD lost her composure, Mason would have continued choking. I want my children and those around me to see themselves as heroic, as noble, as brave, as good people.

You want to actively look for good traits and noble deeds in other people. Train yourself to use positive and supportive language. And when you compliment other people, be sure to be specific about the behavior you are praising. For example, rather than saying "Nice job," I might say, "Hey, you did a tremendous job staying calm in that scary situation! You may just have saved your brother's life." While keeping it sincere, you want to compliment frequently for it takes as many as 10 compliments to undo 1 insult or disparaging remark.

Remind yourself to be generous with your praise to others around you. As long as you are sincere and specific, I don't think you can compliment too much. We tend to get in a routine of taking people for granted and assuming they know how much we love them. Your loved ones have a short memory span. They get afraid. They doubt themselves. *One way to keep this in mind is to treat other people as if they were going to pass away at midnight.* What would you want your loved ones to know today if you knew that you would never have another chance to speak to them again? In general, we tend to be quicker to criticize than compliment. As long as your compliments are heartfelt, I don't think you can go wrong.

Don't Compare Yourself to Others

Comparisons are a recipe for disaster. You are unique. Comparisons are deadly because you can always find someone who is bigger, smarter happier, wealthier or better looking. Rather than long for the waif thin body of a super model, train yourself to be grateful for what you have.

Acquisition is Not the Main Goal of Life

Research studies tell us again and again that money is NOT the key to happiness. Sure, you need a certain amount to support a standard of living. But after that, money provides no additional increase to happiness. Striving after acquisition of material items leaves you lonely and empty at the end of the day. Find other values to complement your life such as helping others, love of learning, spirituality, family and wisdom.

Exercise Daily

Anything that raises your risk of heart disease, such as smoking, obesity, high blood pressure, stress – also increases your risk of losing your memory and darkening your mood. If you want to keep your heart chugging along, if you want to keep your brain in high gear, if you want to be happier, if you want a healthy heart for years to come, stay physically fit. Make it a priority to exercise every day, even if it's only for ten minutes.

Stress and Perception

A large part of creating more happiness in your life revolves around stress management. It's difficult to be happy and carefree when you are bogged down by worries and fears sparked by stress.

Stress is not caused by the event itself. *Stress is caused by your perception of the event.* You have control over how you perceive the world around you. Your perceptions are based upon your interpretations of the world around you – expectations of others, attributions of the motivations of others, and your expected outcomes of situations.

Third, negative emotions are destructive in terms of the behaviors that frequently result from them. Anger and rage in particular cause a great deal of misery to yourself and others.

In short, negative interpretations lead to negative perceptions which create negative emotions. The negative emotions cause the body to dump hormones in the bloodstream which are damaging to the body when they remain at high levels for long periods of time. Negative thoughts and emotions exist simultaneously with stress – the body's response to the disappointment that occurs when your perceptions don't meet your expectations. More specifically, stress occurs when you fail to manage your emotional reaction to this disappointment. Your stress (and negative emotions) may be felt as strain, tension, fatigue, and frustration and can become disabling if it persists for too long.

Re-interpret Stressful Situations

Part of the solution to increasing positive emotional energy is changing how you perceive the stressful situations around you. Research has shown that *it is not the stressful events themselves that cause the stress; it's how we react to these events.* While we cannot control the stressful events around us, we can control our reactions to, or our perceptions of, these events. This is the secret to managing stress.

Stress, and the negative emotional energy that accompanies it, begins with your perception of the situation. By becoming more aware of your perceptions and your reactions to them, you will begin to reduce and eventually eliminate the chronic stress that is so much a part of your life. As incentive, remind yourself that negative emotions such as anger, resentment, sadness, anxiety and worry are toxic to your brain, heart and body. This is true regardless of whether or not these emotions are justified. *Your brain does not recognize the difference between the internal world and the external world.* Your brain reacts in the same manner to a train speeding at you as to a mental picture of an oncoming train (with your eyes closed). The same neural networks in your brain are activated in both situations.

Learn to Forgive

Forgiveness has been thought of in a number of different ways. The way in which you conceive of forgiveness creates or limits your possibilities, your willingness and ability to forgive, and as a result, profoundly affects your emotional well-being.

Forgiveness is the conversion of old negative emotions towards the offending party into new positive emotions. Forgiveness can be a process which encourages the offending party to behave in a more appropriate manner in the future. Forgiveness is primarily a way to rid your self of negative emotions felt towards the offending party such as anger, contempt and disappointment. In addition, you can forgive yourself for being less than perfect or for making mistakes. On top of the positive benefits to forgiving a known offender and yourself, positive benefits accrue from forgiving an unknown offender, groups of people as well as an abstract institution.

Each one of us has an emotional gas tank inside us. Inside most of us, our emotional gas tanks are filled with anger, sadness and fear, or negative emotions. Negative emotions build up over time. They accumulate.

As an example, take anger. Anger is difficult to control yet it is predictable. While anger can come over you like a lightning bolt, it also can accumulate over time. It begins like a single drop of water. At first, it's merely irritating. No big deal, just aggravating. Slowly, gradually, over time, anger accumulates. Some bonehead zips into the parking space for which you were patiently waiting. A guy in a hurry cuts you off on the freeway. Your boss is mistakenly upset with you because of an error a coworker made. The waitress takes forever to get your order and you are running late. When you finally arrive home, exhausted, your children are boisterous and energetic. Tiny drops of water slowly filling up your emotional gas tank. Drip. Drop. Drip. Drop. And when you gather together enough of these little drops of annoyance, you have unknowingly filled your tank with rage and anger. You now jump to judgment. You are fast to fury. You instantly become irritated. Over time, over years and years of this pattern, you learn to trust no one. You learn to expect the worst from people. You build a wall to shield you from more pain. And the quality of your life gradually becomes miserable. It's insidious. Without awareness, you become an emotional time bomb that explodes under the slightest of difficulties.

There is a better way to live. It requires learning the human strength of forgiveness. Forgiveness takes some awareness and practice, but it can be learned.

All you have to do is learn how to dump out your emotional gas tank. Turn it upside down and release every last bit of negative emotions – anger, fear, disappointment and sadness. Once you've emptied your tank, you have the option of filling it up with what you choose – love, joy, peace and patience.

The problem is that no one ever taught you HOW to empty out your gas tank of these destructive emotions. Once you learn how to dump out all that rage and pain, then you have a choice. Then you will have a life of which you can be proud.

The problem is that life is flawed. There is nothing permanent in life. Eventually, everything we love will wither and die. One of the few certainties in life is that, at some point, **everyone** feels heartbroken, let down, betrayed, or disappointed. That is the price we must pay to live life. And it's normal to feel anger, sorrow and fear as a result of terrible events such as homicide, rape or assault. The key is to learn how to get unstuck from those feelings. The less time you spend wallowing in your destructive emotions, the better your quality of life will be.

Why Learn Forgiveness?

We have a lifetime of experience holding on to our hurt. However, no one has ever taught us HOW to release the pain. Research has shown that it *is bad for our bodies* when we dwell on negative feelings. Yet most of us don't know any other way.

Studies show that people with higher levels of anger, fear and depression have more health problems, are more stressed, are at a higher risk of heart disease, have a higher incidence of cancer, are less hopeful and have fewer quality relationships. Negative emotions eat away at the inside of your arteries, are bad for your heart and kill your brain cells. They raise your blood pressure, make your muscles tense and cause more cortisol, the stress chemical, to be released into your body.

Now you know why you want to get rid of those negative, destructive emotions you've been sitting on for decades. Let's look at what forgiveness is and how to start to learn to forgive.

What is Forgiveness?

Learning how to forgive takes some practice. It takes a little open-mindedness. However, it works and it is tremendously powerful. Forgiveness is not for wimps. Forgiveness is not an act of weakness. Forgiving does NOT mean that you approve of the act which broke your heart.

Forgiveness is a human strength. According to Dr. Fred Luskin, Director of the Stanford University Forgiveness Project, "*Forgiveness is the feeling of peace that you have in the present moment when you learn to stop dwelling on past hurts, betrayals and tragedies.*"62 Forgiveness is way to reclaim your power and control over your life. There are five kinds of forgiveness.

5 Types of Forgiveness

1. **Forgiveness of others.** Forgiveness is a gift which you extend to other people who have wronged you. However, here's the catch. Forgiveness is truly done for yourself. Forgiving others their trespasses against you allows you to release your anger, disappointment and sorrow. Forgiveness is done to help you. It is not a weakness. It is a strength that you can learn to develop. Forgiveness is one of the most powerful human strengths you can learn. *Forgiveness is the feeling of peace that you have in the present moment when you learn to stop dwelling on past hurts, betrayals and tragedies.* Forgiveness is done to help YOU out, NOT the offender. Forgiveness is way to reclaim your power and control over your life.

Forgiveness does not mean that you condone of or approve of the wrongdoings that hurt you. You don't need to be face-to-face with the offender in order to forgive. In fact, many times, it may be safer and wiser NOT to forgive the offender face-to-face. In any case, you can forgive anyone all by yourself.

2. **Allowing others to forgive us.** It is just as important to offer forgiveness to others as it is to receive forgiveness yourself. This allows you to release your guilt and self-loathing. Just as you learn to accept an apology

(or a compliment!) with grace and an open heart, you must also learn to accept the genuine forgiveness of other people.

I see this in my children frequently, where I will forgive one of them for breaking a vase, for example, and they don't accept my forgiveness. My older son, in particular, will remain upset at himself for a long time. He beats himself up over his mistakes, long after his mother and I have forgiven him. So I try to teach him how to accept our forgiveness by reminding him of what is truly important and what is not. One way to do this is to ask yourself, "Will this matter a year from now?" If the answer is "No" then let it go. Breathe it out.

3. **Forgiveness of self** allows you to release your need to be perfect, your guilt related to your own shortcomings and your shame, or your belief that you are a bad person at the core. Remember, guilt stems from something you have done which you know to be wrong. Guilt can be productive by steering you away from danger or wrongdoing. Guilt can spur you on to do the right thing. On the other hand, shame develops as a result of something that was done to you at a very early age, something over which you had little to no control. Shame is unproductive.

4. **Forgiveness of God** which as well as

There are two types of forgiveness where God is involved:

1. **You forgiving God** – When you forgive God, you begin to recognize and release any anger you may have at God because it allows you to let go of the idea that life should be fair. Life isn't perfect. It's not SUPPOSED to be. Happiness can only be measured by the depth of our struggles. Without anger, sadness and fear, there would be no joy or pleasure in happiness. For example, my youngest son's soccer team went undefeated last season. And it amazed me how unsatisfying the wins became towards the end of our season. To win became merely expected. Once the expectation was lived up to, there was slight satisfaction that disappeared momentarily. Even the boys weren't all that excited after scoring a goal – it was just one more goal leading to one more win. On the other hand, we are now playing indoor soccer with a much different team. Wins are much harder to come by. Yet, when we do win, the excitement, elation and fulfillment run deep and last longer. To bring it back to my point, our joy is measured by our trials and tribulations. The struggles we endure give us perspective and appreciation of our victories – moral or otherwise. Life is intended to be filled with ups and downs. Forgiveness is a key to bouncing back from the down times.

2. God forgiving you – Asking God to forgive you your mistakes and shortcomings gives you a fresh start. Asking forgiveness of a higher power enables you to let go of your mistakes so you can stay in the present moment rather than fretting over the past or worrying about the future. It is critical to learn to let go of the past. You cannot change the past. It is done. The best you can do is manage your actions, thoughts and feelings in the present moment. Asking God for forgiveness is one way to do just that.

How do you forgive?

Forgiveness begins with the realization that you are in control over how you feel. You have a choice as to whether or not you want to hold on to the anger you feel – anger at those who have wronged you, anger at God, anger at your self, anger at your parents, anger at everybody. Forgiveness is a learnable skill just like learning to swim.

The beliefs that you hold about forgiveness open or close possibilities for you. These beliefs determine your willingness to forgive. As a result, your beliefs about forgiveness dramatically influence how happy you are.

One of the ways that I learned to forgive came with the realization that I only harm myself when I hold on to my anger. It does nothing to get back or to punish the trespasser. Many times the person who wronged you doesn't even *know* you are angry. So your anger has no effect on them.

Also, forgiveness shatters the illusion that you are a victim of your past traumas or mistakes. You are not a victim of your past. You are a survivor. You are the hero of your own story. The past is the past. You cannot change it. The best you can do is to learn new ways of being in the present moment.

Forgiveness is a way out of your prison of pain. Forgiveness is a show of inner strength, NOT weakness. Forgiveness is a sign that you are able to rise above that which life has thrown your way. Forgiveness indicates to others that you have the power to overcome tragedy.

Getting to Forgiveness

Normally, when someone has wronged you, you create mental stories about the injustice done to you. Then you rehearse it over and over again. Many of us get stuck and have a hard time turning the page in our mind.

There are usually three parts to these stories, or grievances:

1. You take the offense too personally (when in fact it usually has little to do with you).
2. You blame the offender for your emotions surrounding the episode.
3. You create a grievance story and dwell on it.

By following these three steps, you can virtually guarantee a drop in life satisfaction, a decline in mood, and greater stress.

Rather than take these three steps, here are three new steps you can learn. The goal is to replace the steps above with the new steps below. As you practice, forgiveness becomes easier and easier. As you consciously think about forgiving others throughout the day, day after day, you start to *become* a forgiving person.

The idea is to retell your story with you as the hero rather than the victim. This means that you have to find some sort of positive lesson or meaning in the tragic event. You want to learn to take things less personally. And you want to realize that you are in charge of your own feelings. No one can make you feel anything you don't want.

Retell the grievance story

1. Take it less personally (i.e., it has NOTHING to do with you)
2. Take responsibility for how you feel
3. Turn yourself into the hero of the story rather than the victim

Start forgiving your self and your loved ones today. It's a process that you learn. It takes time. You will make mistakes. That's okay. Forgive yourself for not being perfect. The more you practice it, the more forgiveness becomes a way of life and the happier you become.

In order to forgive, there are three things you need prior to the act of forgiveness. You need to know exactly how you feel about the situation. You need to know what went wrong. And you need to share it with some close friends.

3 Preconditions to Be Able to Forgive

1. **Know HOW you feel** – Know specifically what emotions you are feeling. Most times in tragic situations, a grieving process takes place. Grieving usually involves anger, disappointment (a combination of anger and sadness), sorrow, and shock.
2. **Know WHAT was wrong** – Know specifically which behaviors were hurtful or which words caused pain.
3. **Tell 1-3 trusted friends what happened** – Share your newly recreated story with some trusted friends.

If none of these suggestions work, pray to your Higher Power to be willing to be willing to forgive the offending party.

Here's one other look at forgiveness as a process. In an article in the *Chronicle of Higher Education* (Heller, 1998), he outlines the following nine steps toward forgiveness which play out over time (it's a process!):

1. Acknowledge your emotions. Whether you are angry, hurt, ashamed, or embarrassed (or some combination of the above), acknowledge your emotional reaction to the wrongdoing.
2. Go beyond identifying the person who hurt you and articulate the specific behaviors that upset or hurt you.
3. Make the conscious choice to forgive.
4. Explain to yourself why you made the decision to forgive. Your reasons can be as practical as wanting to be free of the anger so that you can concentrate better at work.
5. Attempt to "walk in the shoes" of the other person. Consider that person's vulnerabilities. You are not perfect, nor is anyone else.
6. Make a commitment to not pass along the pain you have endured—even to the person who hurt you in the first place.
7. Decide instead to offer the world mercy and goodwill. You may wish to reconcile with the other person (but it's not necessary).

8. Reflect on how it feels to let go of a grudge. Does it feel better to hold on to the hurt or to let it go?
9. Find a positive meaning in the suffering you experienced and overcame.
10. Discover the paradox of forgiveness: As you give the gift of forgiveness to others, you receive the gift of peace.

Another way to let go of anger and disappointment is to write a letter forgiving the individual who has hurt you. You don't need to send the letter. You can tear it or cut it up. This is symbolic of dismantling your anger.

A final suggestion is to use your imagination. I have a friend whose son was murdered in the Oklahoma City bombing many years ago. He has struggled with anger, sadness and resentment for roughly ten years. Recently, he came to understand the power of daily forgiveness. What he does is visualize a shaft of light coming from God to him and then from him to his murderers. And he actively forgives them and sends his love and blessing to them each and every day. I'm not sure this does anything to help or hurt the murderers. Yet it DOES help him to release his anger towards them and get on with his day in a positive and loving manner. The interesting thing is that he has to do it everyday. Those days that he forgets, he finds himself more irritable and quicker to anger.

Practice forgiving yourself for not living up to your expectations, for not being perfect, for being human. On the whole, we are better at forgiving others than we are at forgiving ourselves. To get to self-forgiveness, get on your knees and state out loud, "Right here, right now, I am giving up all my old anger, my old fear, my old sadness. I do not need it any longer. I am giving up all my old negative emotions that I have held onto for so long, so that I may be renewed with positive emotions. I forgive myself for not being perfect. I forgive myself for my anger, my sadness, and my fear. I forgive my family and friends. I ask their forgiveness of me. I forgive God for making an imperfect world. I ask forgiveness from you, God, for my trespasses. Fill me now with the positive energy of love and compassion."

Forgive other people no matter what their transgression is. It may take some time to get to the point where you are willing to forgive depending upon the trespass. However, until you forgive, you carry around accumulated negative emotions which weigh you down and drain your energy. Learn to forgive quickly. It does you no good to hold on to anger and sadness.

> *Ninety percent of the world's woe comes from people not knowing themselves, their abilities, their frailties, and even their real virtues. Most of us go almost all the way through life as complete strangers to ourselves. - Sydney J. Harris*

Laying the Groundwork for Positive Moods

Positive emotions and temperament arise due to intentional thought as opposed to negative emotions which are more likely to arise unexpectedly due to the situation. This means that a positive temperament can be nurtured and encouraged by intentionally thinking about positive emotions. The best positive emotions to dwell on are love and compassion. In this way, you can meet the world with a positive mindset and rid yourself of destructive emotions that obscure your clear vision and well-being.

Emotional energy is the energy gained from fostering positive emotions. It is renewed by thinking about love and compassion. It is minimizing the time you spend wallowing in negative emotions and maximizing the time you spend in positive emotions such as love and compassion.

Adopt the Right Attitude

Part of sustaining you're a positive mood is adopting the proper attitude. The other part is practicing certain exercises that have been shown to have a positive and lasting impact on your thought processes. The proper attitude is one of love and compassion.

When you come right down to it, the secret of having it all is *loving* it all. Unconditional love is the intentional choice to look for the best in people, other living creatures and any part of nature. Other people don't care how much you know until they know how much you care. By noticing the beauty that surrounds us everyday, we can lift up ourselves and others.

> *No one is to be called an enemy; all are your benefactors, and no one does you harm. You have no enemy except yourselves. - St. Francis of Assisi*

Settle for "Good Enough"

Americans have always valued freedom. This has led to a steady increase in autonomy and independence. Currently, many of us have an unprecedented number of choices available to us. You have a choice over what to buy, where to buy it, what to watch, where to go, how to worship, how to parent, how to look, how to act, and who to marry. On one hand, this self-determination and independence is a fantastic opportunity to create, challenge, experiment and learn. On the other hand, the overwhelming array of choices can also be paralyzing and anxiety-provoking.

It is paralyzing because too many choices can work against your well-being. This is due to the anti-intuitive finding that along with your increase in choice comes an unprecedented wave of unhappiness – chronic depression, suicide attempts, and use of psychological services and psychopharmacological drugs.

> To be nobody-but-yourself--in a world which is doing its best, night and day, to make you everybody else--means to fight the hardest battle which any human being can fight; and never stop fighting. - e. e. cummings

How could freedom and choice relate to an increase in unhappiness? Shouldn't it allow for more happiness? Remember where we discussed your rational, thinking brain and your emotional, feeling brain? The answer is that people can ignore undesirable options at a logical level. However, they cannot ignore them on an emotional level.

More options give you opportunities, but it also causes a dilemma that has to be solved. The dilemma is that more choices make you put more mental energy and time into figuring out the best answer for each choice. Choice creates worry – worry over whether or not you made the right choice, worry over whether you got enough information, worry about the possibility of mistakes. You see, choices force you to constantly make tradeoffs between options of differing quality. And this creates anticipation and high expectations. Expectations frequently get so high that they can never be satisfactorily met. This leads to disappointment when the expectations are not met. And in turn, it causes you to blame yourself for making a less than perfect choice.

Obviously, the problem of too many choices is not a problem for everyone. However, it does pose a particularly insidious problem for those who feel like they have to be at the top, to get the best, and to be the best. These are the perfectionists. For perfectionists, too many choices can be traumatic. The only way to truly know if you are getting the best is to explore every other possible option and then rule out all lesser options. This is a poor use of mental energy since in this age of the Internet; there are nearly an infinite number of possibilities to check out before making a decision. This is a sure way to drain your self of mental, emotional and physical energy.

On the other hand, those individuals that are willing to settle for an option that is good enough can stop expending their energy looking. Simply make a "good enough" decision and relax. Coming out of college, the perfectionists get $7,000 more in starting salary. However, the perfectionists reported themselves to be more negative in their outlook, more exhausted, more stressed, more frustrated, more worried, more overwhelmed, and more depressed. *The perfectionists were paid more, but felt worse and enjoyed life less.* Thus, the perfectionists were drained of their mental and emotional energy merely by virtue of their approach to the choices in their lives.

While there are times that you should find and demand the best choice, there are more times that you should be happy with good enough. You may end up with outcomes that are slightly less good, but you will be much more satisfied with life. And you will save yourself a great deal of mental and emotional energy. Only demand the best in matters of utmost importance. This means that you need to be wise in your use of judgment and discernment. Learn to discern when you want to settle for good enough and when you need to demand the best. When in doubt, settle for good enough. You'll be happy you did.

> *Throughout the years of your life you will face many challenges, remember that you can climb the highest mountain, drive through the roughest storm, soar across the bluest sky, or even sail across the roughest waters. It is only destined by your attitude where you will end up in life. The most important thing is don't let yourself get lost in the crowd. - Angela Duvall*

Visualization Exercise

Picture your self as a net through which emotions pass. When I was young, I believed myself to be a container of emotions without really being aware of it. This is a dangerous belief. We are not intended to nor can we contain the power of emotions, particularly negative emotions. You must find a way to let emotions pass through you. Emotions are temporary. They are merely passing by. The feelings you have are just visiting. They are not permanent. They are not intended to be permanent. To help emotions along their way, take a quiet moment and imagine stepping outside of your body and look at yourself as if from above. See yourself standing in a river where the water rushes past your calves. The water is the emotional energy of everything and everyone around you. Most of the water coming at you is negative energy, just as it is in the real world. Now imagine yourself as a fishing net with large gaping holes strung across the river. The holes allow all of the negative energy, or emotion, to pass through you. The net glows golden and acts like a magnet for positive energy. The net attracts and holds onto kind words, happiness and contentment. This positive energy may be used to fill your emotional reservoir to use as you see fit.

> *To do the right thing in the world, first you must know who you are and what gives meaning to your life. - Paula P. Brownlee*

Develop Hardiness

Hardiness is a newly discovered personality trait which helps to ease the negative effects of extreme trauma and stress. Hardiness has four components to it:

1.) A commitment to discovering meaning and purpose in all of life
2.) A core belief that you can positively influence your surroundings and the outcome of situations
3.) A belief that you can learn and grow from both positive and negative situations in life.
4.) A belief in a just world.

Guided by this set of beliefs, hardy people have been shown to interpret potentially stressful events as less frightening. This reduces their experience of stress which minimizes the output of cortisol in their body. Less cortisol means less muscle tension and wear and tear on the body. These individuals are also more confident and more adept at using active coping skills and social supports so they are better able to deal with the stressful situations that they do encounter.

> *Some luck lies in not getting what you thought you wanted, but getting what you have, which once you have got it you may be smart enough to see is what you would have wanted had you known. - Garrison Keillor*

Laugh and Smile

Resilient individuals tend to deal better with trying times through the use of positive emotions and laughter.[63] In the past, laughter and positive emotion in the context of extremely traumatic events was viewed as ineffective or as a form of unhealthy denial. Recently, however, studies have demonstrated that laughter and the cultivation of positive emotion can help reduce levels of distress following traumatic events by quieting and by undoing the effects of negative emotions.[64] In addition, laughter helps by fostering ongoing contact with and eliciting support from important individuals around you. Individuals who laughed and smiled despite a recent death in the family were more likely to be well adjusted over several years of bereavement. Laughter and smiles also predicted better social relationships over time. Remember, laugh easily!

> *To be what we are, and to become what we are capable of becoming, is the only end of life. - Baruch Spinoza*

As emotions are contagious, you want to surround yourself with optimistic, loving people.

Surround yourself with Optimistic and Non-judgmental People

Emotional energy is frequently picked up from other people with whom we live and work. You can "catch" anger, fear and sadness. Emotions are contagious. Optimistic people tend to have more positive emotions. Pessimistic people tend to have more negative emotions.

Think about the last time you were with a friend who was upset.

As they speak of their upsetting experience, you become upset also. This is especially true if you are intuitive and empathic.

Positive emotional energy is seen in those who give off a peaceful feeling. You feel their heart, compassion and grace when you are around them. You feel intuitively relaxed and secure around them. You want to get to know them more. You want to be around them. And your energy and optimism actually increase with them. You feel as if you can do more just by being with them.

With negative energy people, you feel drained of energy. You may feel sick to your stomach. You may feel attacked or defensive. Negative people make you feel on guard, cautious, and tense. Your intuition may pick up sharp, unfriendly vibes that tell you to get away from them – fast. Staying receptive to the positive energy in people is the easy part. Protecting yourself from the negative emotions from other people is much more difficult. I will speak to this in a later book.

> *Start doing the things you think should be done, and start being what you think society should become. Do you believe in free speech? Then speak freely. Do you love the truth? Then tell it. Do you believe in an open society? Then act in the open. Do you believe in a decent and humane society? Then behave decently and humanely. - Adam Michnik*

Learn to be Realistically Optimistic

Let me begin this section by telling you one of my favorite stories called, The Donkey and the Farmer.

One day a farmer's donkey fell into an old well. The donkey whimpered and cried for hours as the farmer tried to figure out what to do. After giving it some thought, the farmer decided that the donkey had lived a long life, the well needed to be covered up anyway, so in the end it just wasn't worth trying to save the donkey.

The farmer decided to bury the donkey.

The farmer invited all of his neighbors over to help shovel dirt into the old well. Everyone grabbed a shovel and began shoveling dirt into the well.

At first, when the donkey realized what was going on, he cried and hee-hawed terribly as he was certain he was going to die. After a few moments, however, the donkey slowly quieted down. Eventually, the farmer and his neighbors didn't hear anything at all.

A few loads of dirt later, the farmer looked down the well to say one final goodbye to the donkey. When he looked down the well, he was amazed at what he saw. With every shovelful of dirt that landed on top of the donkey, he would shake the dirt off his back, and take a step up towards the light.

As the farmer's neighbors kept shoveling dirt on top of the animal, he continued to shake it off and take another step up. Soon enough, everyone was astonished as the donkey was high enough to walk right over the edge of the well and trotted off on his merry way!

What's the point, you ask? The point is that life is just like being stuck in that well. Life throws dirt on you all the time; all kinds of dirt. The trick to being happy and succeeding is to shake off the dirt and use it to take another step up – towards the Light.

Each one of our troubles is a stepping stone, a challenge, a lesson to be learned. We can always manage to get out of the deepest wells by not stopping, by never giving up, by shaking off the dirt and taking a step up.

How you respond to challenges, that is, the dirt that life throws on top of you, is a powerful indicator of how happy you are, how resilient you are and how successful you will be. People with an optimistic attitude see obstacles and setbacks as temporary challenges, challenges that can be overcome with effort. That one attitude of realistic optimism provides the foundation for perseverance and resilience that fuel high achievers. Details on how to become more realistically optimistic can be found in the chapter on healthy mental exercises.

Visualization Exercise

While breathing in a sitting position, picture a long, unbreakable tree trunk or tail stretching down from your spine, anchoring you into the ground. As you breathe, feel your connection with the earth deepen. Visualize the tree trunk extending all the way to the very core of the earth. Allow the positive energy of the earth to rush into you and stabilize you. This is one way of centering yourself. When you are centered, negative emotion from the outside cannot derail or invade you.

Here is another simple visualization exercise. As you exhale, picture negative emotions leaving your body as black smoke. As you inhale, imagine love, energy and forgiveness entering your body as pure, white light.

You can reap tremendous benefits from this exercise while doing it for as little as three minutes

These two exercises are very powerful in helping you to refill your emotional gas tank. And most of us go through our lives with an empty gas tank. While I knew my emotional tank was running on empty for years, I had no real way to refill it. I now use these visualization exercises several times a day to renew my positive emotional energy. Remember your brain doesn't know the difference between what is perceived and what is imagined. Visualization exercises are thus extremely powerful in creating a happier life.

> *There is only one you for all time. Fearlessly be yourself. - Anonymous*

Summary

In summary, people speak of unpleasant emotions twice as much as pleasant emotions.[65] Yet, to lead a thriving life, you must feel pleasant emotions three times as often as negative ones. To the extent that you can stop talking about your negative emotions and foster positive feelings, you will enjoy the sense of security and belonging that all of us crave. Full emotional energy is accompanied by a calm, secure and balanced feeling. It is marked by a greater awareness of your intuition. The head (mental) may know but the heart (emotional) understands. As your emotional energy and awareness grow, so will your feelings of love, compassion, understanding, patience, tolerance and forgiveness. These feelings are frequently accompanied by a relaxed state of awareness in which everything becomes clearer. Additionally, when we have sufficient emotional energy, our thought processes slow down, become more rational and focused. Our understanding, problem-solving ability and creativity all increase. We have a feeling of being in control and we see life from a more optimistic and hopeful place.

> *"I have learned that success is to be measured not so much by the position that one has reached in life as by the obstacles which he has overcome while trying to succeed." Booker T. Washington*

The Rational Mind

Mental energy is made up of your thoughts, beliefs and attitudes. It is the self-talk that runs through your head when you silently converse with yourself. Researchers state that you have approximately 50,000 thoughts pass through his or her head each and every day. And 80% of this self-talk is negative. I'm sure you're familiar with it. Negative thoughts sound like this…

"I'm so stupid."
"I'll never be a good father!"
"I'm not a good person."
"I'm a failure."
"Everyone hates me."
"I'll never lose this weight."
"I know they're talking about me."
"I'm over the hill."
"I am so out of shape."
"I just don't have the energy that I used to."
"I've never been good at that."
"Why do I always get in the slowest line?!"
"I'm a burden on my loved ones. They are better off without me."
"I can't take any more of this."
"I can't trust anyone around here."
"Nothing ever goes right for me."
"I wish I'd never been born."
"I'm at the end of my rope. I can't do this any longer."
"I hate myself."
"If only I were smarter… taller… thinner… wealthier…"
And so on.

Watch Out for Gremlin Thinking

A Gremlin is a negative thought such as, "I don't deserve happiness because I'm unworthy."

Pastor Mice Bucholtz, author of *"Smelly Socks"* calls such negative, self-defeating thoughts the "Itty-Bitty-Shitty-Committee" as it's that part of your mind that points out how wrong you are, how lousy life is and how untrustworthy other people are. I call negative thoughts 'Gremlins.' This helps me to approach my negative thoughts as a game. The goal of the game is to police your mind so that Gremlin thoughts don't loiter long. Gremlins that do sneak in are promptly pounced on and thrown out by Gremlin Police. Even as I write this, my Gremlins are telling me "This book is too much. You can't finish it." Yet when I become aware of them, I can defend myself. I can lock them up in Gremlin prison. I can smack them with a mental flyswatter. I can counter them with positive thoughts.

One of the most amazing principles discovered by neuroscience is that "imagery activates and stimulates the same brain systems as does real perception."[66] This is a principle I'll return to throughout the book because it has tremendous implications for what and how we perceive life around us. Multiple studies have confirmed that *imagining* an object, such as a child in a troll costume, uses the same neural substrates as *looking* at a child dressed in a troll outfit. This means that the power of your thoughts has far more potential to help and harm than most ever realize. Imagery and visualization exercises have been shown to reduce pain by up to 63%[67], to accomplish difficult goals and to improve physical performance.

Your mind is constantly under attack by your own negative thoughts.

As I mentioned before, researchers estimate that we have roughly 50,000 thoughts sneaking through our minds daily. I don't know who is counting these thoughts, but they estimate that 80% of our thoughts are negative and self-punitive. And you are not even aware of most of these thoughts. Take a moment and ponder the weight of that idea.

Think of the influence that 40,000 negative thoughts have on you each and every day. That's 40,000 Gremlins running through your head each and every day. That's a mob scene! You are under siege by Gremlins and you may not even know it.

Now multiply 40,000 by 365 and you have roughly 14,600,000 negative thoughts that you tell yourself each year of your life. Fourteen million negative messages per year! Now let's assume that you are 40 years old. Before your forty-first birthday, you have experienced over 550 million negative thoughts. So you've told yourself, for example, that you're worthless, stupid, no good, selfish, greedy, ugly and overweight hundreds of millions of times before you turn forty one. Each one of those thoughts leaves a faint little imprint on your brain. And each time the thought is repeated that imprint gets a little deeper, a little more real, and a little harder to shake.

At what point, does self-flagellation become unproductive? At what point do you fall awake? When do you start becoming aware of your inner mental landscape and the characters and messages that populate it? When does the madness stop? When is enough -- enough?

Hundreds of scientific studies clearly demonstrate that our physical body is affected by our thoughts. We know this from functional MRIs, SPECT brain scans, PET scans, as well as physiological changes such as perspiration on finger tips, heart rate, breathing rate, and chemical changes within the body.[68,69,70,71]

Negative thoughts affect your body in a negative manner. They steal your confidence. They increase your anger. They rob your patience. They convince you that you are unworthy. They make you believe that you cannot. And they drain you of your energy. I'll discuss the various types of Gremlin thinking in more detail later in this book.

Positive thoughts affect you in a positive manner. They make you more creative, happier, content, creative and peaceful. Positive thoughts slow your heart rate, speed your recovery from negative situations and make you more resilient.

> *"Every man is enthusiastic at times. One man has enthusiasm for thirty minutes, another man has it for thirty days, but it is the man who has it for thirty years who makes a success in life."*
> *Edward B. Butler*

The Full Reservoir

A full reservoir of mental energy leads to greater clarity of thought, greater creativity, better performance, stronger focus, a greater ratio of successes to failures, more flexibility of thought, and realistic optimism grounded in your past successes. You use up your mental energy by thinking negative thoughts, focusing on the same task for more than two hours, shallow breathing, and being overwhelmed by stress.

You gain mental energy by becoming aware of your Gremlin thoughts and rewriting them as positive and supportive. You create more cognitive energy by consciously redirecting your attention from negative thoughts towards positive thoughts. What you believe leads to your attitudes. Your attitudes create thought and feelings. Those thoughts and feelings determine how you act. And your action, or inaction, leads to results. So it's critical to identify your core beliefs. Once you are aware of them, you can begin to reprogram them from negative to positive.

Here are some negative thoughts rewritten as positives:

Gremlin Thoughts	Positive Thoughts
"I'm so stupid."	*"I am smart and capable."*
"I'll never be a good father!"	*"I am a good father. I'm learning daily."*
"I'm not a good person."	*"I am a good person. Sometimes I make mistakes."*
"I'm a failure."	*"I am a success. Failure is a learning opportunity."*

"Everyone hates me."	*"People like to be around me. Don't take it personally."*
"I'll never lose this weight."	*"I am fit due to good eating habits and daily exercise."*
"I know they're talking about me."	*"I cannot control other people. I can manage myself."*
"I'm over the hill."	*"Fifty is the new forty. I take care of my body regardless of age."*
"I am so out of shape."	*"I take good care of myself by exercising and eating right."*
"I've never been good at that."	*"There is no time like the present to learn something new."*
"Why do I always get in the slowest line?!"	*"'Always' is never correct. I'm exaggerating. It's no big deal."*
"I'm a burden on my loved ones."	*"My family loves me no matter what."*
"I can't take any more of this."	*"This is a challenge put before me to test my mettle."*
"I can't trust anyone around here."	*"Some folks are untrustworthy. Most people are basically good."*
"Nothing ever goes right for me."	*"This was a difficult setback. I'll do better next time."*
"I wish I'd never been born."	*"While it may be difficult now, this too will pass."*
"If only I were…"	*"I am bright, cheerful, energetic and full of great ideas."*

Your mental energy grows though the use of your imagination and visualization exercises. These will be discussed later on in this chapter. Mental energy is replenished through deep breathing, relaxation exercises, stretching and exercise.

Mental energy is made up of those functions which take place in the brain and the mind – your cognitive processes. The mind is a phenomenon which emerges from the brain. That is, the mind is more than the sum of its parts. The mind emerges from the complex interactions of billions of neurons and cannot be reduced to mere anatomy.

The mind may be divided into two parts – emotional and rational. While the emotional mind works in an associative manner, the rational mind works in a linear and logical manner. The primary functions of the rational mind are to analyze, plan, reflect upon, memorize, prioritize, compare and sort incoming data from our senses and prior experiences and arrange that data into meaningful chunks, such as perceptions, thoughts, and feelings. The rational mind helps us to make sense of past, current and future situations by using data from our past experiences as well as sensory data. The emotional mind has been developed to protect your body from harm, scan the immediate surroundings for danger, help you to overcome obstacles, and keep you safe when you have lost something or someone close to you.

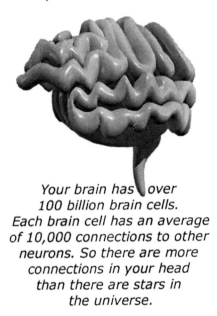

Your brain has over 100 billion brain cells. Each brain cell has an average of 10,000 connections to other neurons. So there are more connections in your head than there are stars in the universe.

Of course, the brain also regulates many of our bodily functions. The brain is the most complex system known to humankind. It contains over one hundred billion neurons, or brain cells. When put together end-to-end, there are more than 2 miles of brain cells in your head. Each brain cell has an average of ten thousand connections to other brain cells. That means that there are more connections in your brain than there are stars in the universe.

The simple fact that there is more of anything in my head and that it works even remotely correctly is absolutely awe-inspiring to me. The fact that I can communicate with you by writing or speaking and you can understand what I am conveying is amazing. To me, this is perhaps the greatest proof of a higher power – that there are more connections in my brain than there are stars in the universe and that I can move my body, laugh, run, and speak is truly a miracle and a gift.

However, the brain does not work perfectly. The brain artificially pieces together a respectable version of reality by analyzing and reconstructing millions of pieces of partial truths and incomplete sensory data. Given the complexity of the task, the brain does an admirable job of creating a somewhat cohesive representation of reality. Yet, it's not perfect. Our perception of reality is not 100% accurate. There is a great deal of room for operator error and individual interpretation.

Your senses take in over 4 million bits of information per second. *You are aware of only 2,000 of those 4 million bits.* These 2,000 tiny pieces of information are filtered and selected based upon your preconceived notions, judgments, emotions, and thoughts.

Think about that for a moment. You are aware of less than 1 percent of the total information that comes in through your senses. So *what* you pay attention to matters enormously in terms of how you view the reality around you. Another way of looking at this is that you create your own reality by what you attend to, how well you manage your emotions, and the content of your thoughts.

Your senses take in over 4 million bits of information per second and you are only aware of 2,000 of them!

By focusing on certain situational elements (e.g., "I'm running late."), cultivating a particular outlook (e.g., "People are out to get me.") and holding on to old ways of thinking (e.g., "Life is meaningless."), you create one reality. This is probably the reality that you are in right now. However, this is only one version of reality out of many.

By changing your outlook (e.g., from pessimistic to optimistic), or by discovering more optimistic ways of thinking (e.g., meaning exists in every situation), or by focusing on situations in a new way, you can literally change the world around you. For instance, you are waiting in line at the bank and the line is moving painfully slowly. You can choose to focus your thinking on elements that will worsen or improve your emotional state. Thoughts that typically will worsen your emotional state include the following:

"This always happens to me."
"I am going to be late for my meeting."
"I don't have time for this."
"I am not putting up with this anymore. I am changing banks."

On the other hand, these thoughts will *improve* your emotional state while waiting in line:

"This line isn't a big deal. I can wait."
"I'll take this time to focus on my breathing."
"I'm sure the bank teller is working as quickly as he can."
"If I'm a few minutes late for the meeting, it won't be the end of the world."

By changing your thoughts, you can create new versions of reality for yourself. You can cultivate optimism, remind yourself to slow down and breathe, calm yourself, and negate catastrophic thoughts.

Is There One Objective Reality?

It is my belief that there is not merely one objective reality. There are actually billions of different realities because each one of us creates our own version based on our unique set of prior experiences and tendencies. The experiences, feelings and attitudes which you bring to the situation shape and filter your view of reality.

I recently did a presentation on realistic optimism for the executives of a large bank. During my presentation, I mentioned that there are numerous realities based on how individuals interpret the situation around them. The VP of Human Resources challenged this saying that there is only one reality. I asked him if he'd even been involved in the investigation of a sexual harassment claim. He replied that he had. I asked him if the two versions of what took place in the harassment case were the same or different. He said they were worlds apart. I said, "I rest my case. Reality is subjective. It is based upon our interpretation and our interpretations are always changing based on our thoughts, feelings, mood, and other factors." This is a hard notion for many folks to wrap their head around. It's a scary idea for some. And that's okay. I'm not claiming that I know the ultimate reality. I'm merely saying that interpretation of any situation will differ tremendously by individual. I'll get into this in a little more detail later.

Top 10 Warning Signs That You Are Crazy (Humor)

1. You start out each morning with a 30-minute jog around the bathroom.
2. You write to your mother in Denmark every week, even though she sends you mail from Ohio asking why you never write.
3. You wear your boxers on your head because you heard it will ward of evil alien spirits.
4. You begin to stop and consider all of the blades of grass you've stepped on as a child, and worry that their ancestors are going to one day seek revenge.
5. You have meaningful conversations with your toaster.
6. Your father pretends you don't exist, just to play along with your little illusion.
7. You put tennis balls in the microwave to see if they'll hatch.
8. Your dentist asks you why each one of your teeth has your name etched on it and you say it's for security reasons.
9. You tend to agree with everything your mother's dead uncle tells you.
10. You argue with yourself about which is better, to be eaten by a koala or to be loved by an infectious disease.

How Thoughts Work

Every time you have a thought, your brain releases chemical and electrical messengers which race through your brain.

When you have a negative thought, your brain releases negative chemicals, such as cortisol, that activate your deep limbic system and make your body feel tense, painful, sweaty, and increase your heartbeat. Your limbic system lies inside the temporal lobes near the center of the brain. The deep limbic system is about the size of a walnut and helps to set the emotional tone of an individual. A less active limbic system is generally associated with a positive and optimistic state of mind. An overactive limbic system usually leads to negativity and irritability.

When you have a positive thought, your brain releases a different set of chemicals, such as DHEA, which acts to clean up cortisol, slow the heart and relax the muscles.

Some people's limbic systems are permanently set to an overactive state. These individuals interpret the world around them through a negative lens. These people interpret both positive and neutral events *in a negative light*. If this condition is never addressed, it is a safe bet that such individuals will lead negative, pessimistic, and less fulfilling lives.

Inspirational Story: Who You are Makes a Difference

A High School teacher wanted to honor each of her senior students by telling them the difference each of them had made to her. She called each student to the front of the room, one at a time. She told each of them how they had made a difference to her and their classmates. Then she gave each one a blue ribbon, embossed with gold letters, which stated, "Who I Am Makes a Difference."

Afterwards, the teacher assigned a class project to see what kind of effect such recognition would have on the community. She handed three more blue ribbons to each student and instructed them to go out and pay it forward to others in their community. The students were told to follow up on the results, see who was received the ribbons, and report back to the class in two weeks.

One of the students went to a manager in a nearby software firm, and recognized the manager for helping him with his career planning. He presented him with the blue ribbon and pinned it on his shirt. Then, he gave the manager two extra ribbons and said, "We're doing a class project on appreciation, and we'd like for you to find one other person to honor, give them their blue ribbon. Then give them the extra ribbon so they can recognize a third person, to continue our recognition project." He then asked the manager to report back to him afterwards so he could share it with the class.

Later that same day, the manager went in to see his superior, who was generally regarded as a negative and grouchy person. The manager told his superior that he respected him tremendously for his creative ingenuity. The superior appeared quite surprised. The manager asked his boss if he would accept the blue ribbon. His surprised boss said, "Well, okay." The manager pinned the blue ribbon right on his boss's sports jacket, near his heart.

As he gave him the final extra ribbon, he asked, "Would you take this last ribbon, and pay it forward by honoring somebody else. The student who initially gave me these ribbons is doing a project for class, and we want to keep this appreciation project going to find out how it affects others."

That evening, the boss came home to his 15-year-old son, and sat down with him. He told his son, "The most amazing thing happened to me at work today. I was sitting in my office, and one of the mid-level managers came in. He told me he admired me and presented me with a blue ribbon for being so creative. Who would have thought?! He thinks I'm incredibly creative! Then he put this blue ribbon on my jacket that says, "Who I Am Makes a Difference." He gave me one additional ribbon and asked me to find someone else to honor with it. While I was coming home tonight, I began thinking about who to honor with this ribbon, and I thought about you. I want to show my admiration for you. My days are really busy and I get very tired and when I come home, I know I don't pay much attention to you. Sometimes I yell at you for not doing your homework and for messing up your bedroom. But for some reason, this evening I just wanted to let you know that you do make a difference to me. Along with your mother, you are the most important two people in my life. My life would be meaningless without you. And I want you to know that I think you are a wonderful person, and I love you!"

The startled teenager broke out in tears and began to sob. His whole body trembled with sadness. He gazed up at his father and mumbled through his tears, "Dad, earlier today I wrote a letter to you and Mom, telling you why I had killed myself, and asking for your forgiveness and understanding. I was going to kill myself tonight with your gun after you fell asleep. I didn't think that you cared about me. The letter is upstairs. I don't think I need it after all." His father went upstairs into his son's bedroom and found a heartfelt letter full of anger, sadness and pain.

The boss went back to work a changed man. He was no longer a grouch. He made sure to tell all his employees that they made a difference to him. The manager helped many other high school students with their career planning, and always remembered to let them know what a difference they made in his life. And the student and his classmates learned a valuable lesson, "*Who you are does make a difference.*"

And who you are is largely determined by how well your brain is working. The brain affects everything you are and everything you do - your emotional well-being, your relationships, work, parenting, marriage, and even your relationship with a higher power. To understand yourself and those around you, you must understand your brain. If your brain is working right, then you are working right.[72]

Event Tagging

Your limbic system "tags" your perceptions and essentially labels them as one of three types – positive, negative or neutral. This tagging of events as positive, negative or neutral is critical to your survival. The weight that you place on a person or event can drive you to act, such as asking someone on a date, or it can cause you to avoid people or behaviors, such as avoiding an ex-wife. In addition, it may cause you to freeze and do nothing such as when you are being judged or evaluated by someone whom you consider superior in some way.

A study done at the National Institute of Mental Health (NIMH) focused on emotional tagging of thoughts. The brain activity of ten normal women was monitored under 3 different conditions. Researchers recorded their brain activity when they were thinking neutral thoughts, positive thoughts, or negative thoughts. The group thinking neutral thoughts showed no signs of changes in the brain. The group told to think positive thoughts demonstrated less activity in the limbic system of their brains. The limbic system became aroused and highly active in those ladies who were thinking negative thoughts. Thus, just the mere fact that these individuals were thinking a positive or negative thought was sufficient to change the functioning of their brains. This is true proof that your thoughts matter!

Your thoughts can even alter the physical make-up of the cells within your body. For instance, if you think you are fat, then existing cells in the body create sister and daughter cells with more fat receptors on them, meaning that they have a greater likelihood of latching on to fat cells. So, to some extent, you can actually think yourself fat!

Here is a brief demonstration for you…

Think about the last time *you felt happy; I mean really, truly happy.* I want you to picture that scene in your mind right now. How did your body feel? What did you smell? Who was there? What were you wearing? How was the weather? Think about the situation in as much detail as you can.

Now, how does your body *feel?*

Thinking back upon a happy time in your life brings up a happy feeling in your body. Your heart rate slows, you breathing deepens, your hands stay dry, and you become more open to new ideas.

Ultimately, you want to create a *mental scrapbook* in your head of a time when you were happy, a time when you were excited, a situation where you felt extremely confident, a time when you were in 'the zone,' and a stressful incident where you remained calm. That way, when you want to access that feeling to enhance your performance, you simply have to think about that photo in your mental scrapbook to bring about the emotion you want.

Let me give you an example. Today, I went in for an MRI scan on my hip for sciatica which I've dealt with for several years. When I booked the appointment, a few days ago, the receptionist asked if I was claustrophobic. Without thinking, I replied, "No." This morning I went in to get the MRI. I lay down on the table which began slowly sliding into the closed, narrow MRI tube. The tube was as wide as my shoulders. I could not move my arms except to fold my hands on my hips. The ceiling of the tube was two inches from my face. As I needed an MRI of my hip, I was slid all the way inside – head first.

I am happy when I think about being on the beach in Maui!

To my surprise, my emotional mind went back to when I was 7 years old trapped in a mummy sleeping bag. And I began to panic. My heart began to race. My fear jumped up into my throat. The emotional side of me wanted to go Incredible Hulk and tear apart the machine which imprisoned me. However, my rational mind knew I had 20 minutes to spend in this tube. So I closed my eyes and reminded myself to breathe deeply. That helped a little. Then I forced myself to smile – a real Duchenne smile using the muscles around my eyes. That helped a little more. Next, I used the mental scrapbook exercise. I thought about the time I came face to face with an ancient sea turtle while snorkeling. I thought about playing with my boys on the beach; and the joyous, toothless, open-mouthed grin of my baby girl; and the birth of my first child. And after that, I relaxed. I began thinking about this book and came up with a new metaphor for the mind – *alligator wrestling*.

It may sound strange at first but it works well as a metaphor. The mind is like a person wrestling an alligator where the person is the rational, conscious part of the mind and the alligator is the emotional, unconscious, automatic part of the mind. Roughly 600 million years ago, the first groupings of brain cells began to evolve in certain organisms. These early brains must have provided some advantage to these organisms because those are the ones that continued to exist and multiply. Brains are adaptive for animals as they automatically and rapidly integrate data from the senses and the environment to allow them to react to perceived dangers. In other words, animals with brains stayed alive longer.

Make a mental scrapbook of the good times. Think of them when you need a boost in mood!

The human brain has developed over millions of years. Its development is similar to adding scoops to an ice cream cone. The brain started off with three scoops: a hindbrain (closest to the spinal cord), a midbrain, and a forebrain (to receive data from the senses). Gradually, more ice cream was added to the top of the cone. In other words, the brain continued to evolve with most of the growth coming in the forebrain area. The limbic system was the fourth scoop and primarily included the hypothalamus (involved in the management of emotions, sexual activity, body temperature, hunger and thirst, and circadian cycles), the hippocampus (plays a critical role in memory and spatial navigation), and the amygdala (serves an important role in the processing of emotions, particularly fear and pleasure). In general, the **limbic system** is involved in the processing of emotion, internal motivation, and emotional memory. Studies have shown that the limbic system is more active in extroverts and risk-takers than in introverts and cautious people. The limbic system has been called the lizard brain as it is the source of our animalistic, primal desires and appetites.

To return to the alligator wrestling metaphor, your emotions are just like the alligator. The alligator sits, just under the surface of the water, waiting for prey to come along. When prey comes, the alligator flashes out of the water, snaps its jaws shut, and pulls the prey into the water. Emotions work very similarly. Emotions hit us quickly, pounce without warning, and are primal and atavistic.

Over time, the brain evolved to include five layers. The final layer is known as the cortex. The cortex is the outer layer of the brain and enables you to plan, organize, set goals, delay gratification and prioritize. In our analogy, the cortex is the person wrestling the alligator. The cortex plays a critical role in managing the base animal impulses that arise from the limbic system. The goal is to train your Crocodile Hunter and the alligator to work together and coexist.

Back to happiness and the powerful impact that thoughts have on your body. Happiness causes your muscles to relax, your hands to become dry, your heart rate to slow, your immune system to function better and breathing to deepen and slow. The point is that your body reacts to EVERY THOUGHT YOU HAVE!

This means that your life will be happier to the extent that you fill your head with positive thoughts and eliminate negative thoughts. To accomplish this, think about what information goes into your head throughout your day.

Talk radio? Turn the dial.

Nightly news? Turn the channel.

Newspaper headlines? Turn to the comics section.

Hateful people? Go elsewhere.

The human brain is plastic. This means that the brain can be molded. Your brain is extremely receptive to suggestion and outside messages. In fact, it's so impressionable; one study showed that years of Coke and Pepsi commercials literally change the physical make-up of your brain. That is frightening! The tiniest thought makes an impression upon your brain. The least amount of suggestion gets written onto it. Every piece of information to which you are exposed gets imprinted onto your brain. Every commercial, conversation, radio show, song lyrics; soap opera anger-filled tirade and talk show sob-story is recorded in the neurons that make up your brain. The more you listen to negative material, the more your brain becomes convinced that the world, and everyone in it, is heartless, cruel and meaningless. All those negative messages normalize and simultaneously perpetuate the insanity.

Stop reading the news section which is constantly filled with mean-spirited acts that we do to one another. Protect yourself from nasty life leeches who put you down and steal your vitality. Start putting positive people and messages in your world today.

> *"Whatever is true, whatever is honorable, whatever is just, whatever is pure, whatever is lovely, whatever is gracious ... think about these things." Philippians 4:8*

Thoughts are **powerful**. They can make your mind and body feel good OR bad. That is why so many physical symptoms, such as stomach aches and headaches, are manifestations of stuffed emotions.

As mentioned before, the brain gathers and combines millions of bits of incomplete and inconsistent data to create a relatively stable pattern of reality. *The brain relies on patterns every minute of every day to make sense of the world.* This is helpful in that you don't have to relearn everything everyday. It saves time and energy.

The Down Side of Pattern Recognition

However, this reliance on pattern recognition has a down side. The brain can get overly reliant on old patterns. Rather than offer creativity and a fresh perspective, *the brain assumes a great deal* about people, places and things around us, including your self. Your brain assumes a great deal about the past and the future. It automatically fills in gaps in knowledge with assumptions based on the current context and your present thoughts and feelings.[73] The brain can be stubborn and insist that it knows reality based on these assumptions. This mindset keeps you from learning, creating, and questioning old ways of thinking. When one adopts a closed mind, all new information has to conform to one's existing version of reality. Data which does not fit into this view of reality is ignored.

> "What you think means more than anything else in your life. More than what you earn, more than where you live, more than your social position, and more than what anyone else may think about you." *George Matthew Adams*

Just like when you were a child, some people act overly aggressive and rob you of precious energy.

How Mental Energy is Spent

Your mental energy is depleted in a variety of ways such as all-or-nothing thinking, emotional reasoning, and always-or-never thinking. Below are some of the main ways that I've seen mental energy "leaking" from my clients. The major culprits responsible for reduced mental energy are a variety of types of negative thoughts, a.k.a. Gremlins.

Negative Thoughts

The thoughts that go through your mind, seemingly every moment, have a profound impact on how your brain works. Research by Mark George, MD and colleagues at the National Institute of Health have shown that happy, hopeful thoughts have an overall calming effect on the brain and body, while negative thoughts fired up those areas in the brain that are involved with depression and anxiety. Your thoughts are powerful. Not only can they change your brain chemistry, they can affect your physical make-up as well. If you think of yourself as "fat", you brain sends electrical and chemical transmissions to your body that causes existing cells to create sister and daughter cells that have more receptors for fat molecules. These new cells are therefore more likely to catch and hold fat molecules. Thus, to some extent, you can literally think yourself fat.

Negative thoughts come from many different sources. Some negative thoughts come from your childhood ("You're worthless! You're a spoiled, little brat! What are you – stupid?"). Others come from people who are full of negative emotional energy. These sorts of people are usually very willing to share (i.e. dump) their negative energy on other people. Some negative thoughts begin at work or at school. It mainly depends upon how successful or frustrated you are in certain situations. The more frustrated you are in a certain setting, the more likely you will spawn habitual negative thoughts.

The Dark Side of the Mind - 'The Gremlin'

Let's talk more in depth about *negative thoughts or 'Gremlins.'* It seems to make it easier for adults as well as children to become aware of, talk about and challenge their negative thoughts. One of the troublesome things about Gremlins is that they have a funny way of growing from one situation to your whole life. For example, let's pretend that you have difficulty in a math class. You begin to think, "I'm stupid." While this thought began in math class, and is related to math in particular, the Gremlin takes on a life of its own and generalizes to your entire being. So it begins in a specific area, such as "I'm stupid in math" and grows into an overgeneralization, such as "I'm a stupid person."

I often teach my clients how to challenge each and every one of their automatic negative thoughts. They pass through your mind quickly and quietly. They happen on their own. But they have tremendous destructive potential. They usually start in childhood and are carried into adulthood. Left unchallenged, these negative thoughts are believed unconditionally by the individual. This is critical to understand. If you do not challenge your negative thoughts, you will believe them, and they will negatively impact your life and your perception of reality.

Your thoughts do not always tell the truth. At times, they flat out lie to you! Most people do not know that thoughts can be deceitful and that they must challenge and dispute their negative thoughts. Most of us don't even think about our thoughts. So people go through life believing whatever irrational thoughts pass through their head. This means that their behavior is based on false beliefs, illogical views and incorrect assumptions. This, in turn, leads to difficulties with moods, behaviors and interpersonal relations. Often these negative thoughts fuel anxiety, depression, anger and misunderstandings. Unfortunately, the development and mastery of our thoughts and feelings is left largely to chance since there is no real curriculum to address these areas in the U.S. public school system.

When your mind is weighed down by too many negative thoughts, it adversely affects your ability to think clearly, to learn, to relate well to other people, and your health. Teaching people how to dispute their negative thoughts is essential if they are to reach their potential and live a satisfying and meaningful life. You want to be aware whether your thoughts are helpful or hurtful and challenge the hurtful ones.

The good news is that you can learn to train your thoughts to be positive, nurturing and supportive. You can choose to think positive, optimistic thoughts, while simultaneously negating negative ones. When you dispute your negative thoughts, you take away its power. This will improve the way you feel.

The trick is to notice your thoughts as they flash through your head. This takes practice and time. However, it is a life-altering skill that is necessary if you want to improve the quality of your life and your level of mental energy.

There are at least ten different kinds of Gremlin species. Gremlins are ways in which your mind distorts incoming information to make you feel lousy and worthless. Think of them as ways in which your mind lies to you with the intent of making the situation worse than it really is.

The Ten Types of Gremlins

Here are the ten types of Gremlins:

1. Mind Reading Gremlin

The Mind Reading Gremlin misleads you into believing you know what another person is thinking and what's more, the other person is thinking something bad about you. Of course all this is concluded without any confirmation of this from the other person. The Mind Reading Gremlin arbitrarily makes the decision that someone is negatively judging you, without bothering to confirm it by any means.

"She didn't email me this morning. She must not love me anymore!"

The Mind Reading Gremlin sounds like this:

"Oh, she just gave me a nasty look. I'll bet she's mad because I came into work five minutes late."

Or "They were just talking about me. I know it."

Pretend that you are headed to a job interview. Your father knows the president of this company. You tell yourself, "I'm only getting this interview because my dad knows the president." In this example, you are assuming that you know how the interviewer is thinking.

Keep in mind that you cannot read anyone else's mind. If you are confused or suspect something, ask for clarification.

One of the most powerful concepts I've learned over the years is that many of us think that 99% of what other people do is a direct result of something we've done, said or thought. In truth, only 1% of what other people do is directly related to something we have done. The other 99% of how others behave is a result of their own emotional baggage which has nothing to do with you. For example, a negative look from your boss may mean nothing more than he or she ran into a lot of traffic on the way to work. You don't know. You can't read minds. I have over 14 years of training in human behavior and I still can't read minds.

2. Fortune Telling Gremlin

The Fortune Telling Gremlin foretells a bad outcome to a situation before it has taken place. To some extent, your mind creates self-fulfilling prophecies. Unconsciously predicting failure will often increase your chances of failing. For example, before talking with your boss about an important client, "I know my boss won't like what I have to say," then you are likely to become anxious during your talk and your brain freezes.

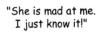
"She is mad at me. I just know it!"

One of the problems with the fortune-telling Gremlin is that as soon as it crosses your mind, it stirs up your anxiety and causes more stress. This guy truly hurts your chances of feeling happy. His job is to look for the worst possible outcome and then try to make you believe it's going to come true. Don't fall for it.

Here is another example of the Fortune Telling Gremlin. You are heading into an important business presentation, and your mind tells you "I'm going to screw it up. My mind will go blank. I won't know what to say." This is Fortune Telling Gremlin predicting something bad will happen without any confirmation from the outside world. This Gremlin is one of the most common and frequently leads to anxiety and fear. Remind yourself that you can't foresee the future. If you *could*, you *would* have invested in the dot coms and got out before the bubble burst.

3. Always or Never Gremlin

The Always or Never Gremlin arises whenever you think words such as "always", "never", "no one", "everything" or "everyone." These thoughts are absolutes. Absolutes are rarely true!

Be careful! The Always or Never Gremlin can negatively influence how you act. For example, my son will get angry and yell "You never let me have my way." Well with that attitude, he's right. But the statement itself isn't true. He does get his way. He just doesn't feel that's true at that moment. You can see the Always or Never Gremlin very clearly in children.

"No one is 'always' stupid or idiotic!"

"I'll always be an idiot!"

This Always or Never Gremlin sounds like this:

"My mom never gave me any attention."
"My children never behave."
"I will never get a raise."
"Why do they always have to disobey me?"
"My friends never call me."

The Always or Never Gremlin is into self-pity. Fortunately, this Gremlin is relatively easy to challenge once you become aware of him. Just remind yourself that the words "always" and "never" don't work well in the real world. Just talk back to this Gremlin. Tell him that the thought isn't really true.

4. Guilt Gremlin

The Guilt Gremlin crops up when you tell yourself that things SHOULD be a certain way, the way you hoped or expected them to be. After doing some on-air coaching, *my* guilt Gremlin might tell me something like, "Gee John, you *should* have said this. Why didn't you say that? You ought to be more relaxed. You have to give better advice." And so on.

If you believe the Guilt Gremlin, he can keep you tied up for days, feeling badly. Statements that include words like "should" and "ought" which are directed against you, only lead to frustration, guilt and diminished performance. Statements that contain "should" or "ought" and are directed at others, generally lead to frustration and anger because you cannot control other people. So to slap a "should" statement on them is only going to lead to a rule which is unenforceable and out of your control. It usually winds up making you angry when things don't work out like you think they "should".

A number of us try to motivate ourselves with "should" and "ought" statements as you were a misbehaving child. Statements like "I shouldn't eat that piece of cake" rarely work well. The statement makes you feel rebellious and you are struck by the urge to do just the opposite. It's like telling someone "DON'T sit down." When you're told, "Don't sit down", you automatically want to sit down. It's human nature. You're much better off phrasing statements positively. So instead of saying "Don't sit down", it's more effective to say "Stand up."

Guilt Gremlins come around when you get overwhelmed by thoughts such as...

"I have to watch my children on Saturday. " In this case, you can change the wording to "I get to..."

"I should have spent more time at work yesterday." Leave the past in the past. Focus on the present.

"I must call my mother."

"I ought to clean the house."

This Gremlin makes me think of an angry parent shaking a finger at you. The key words to watch for are "should," "ought," "have to," and "must." These are the calling cards of the Guilt Gremlin. They often herald an unenforceable rule which is a rule that cannot be enforced. Thus, when it's broken, you feel badly – typically anger, sadness or stress. The result is that you often feel pressured, nervous, resentful and not good enough. Remind yourself that guilt is not a productive emotion unless it spurs you onto productive action. Guilt Gremlins are happiest when you dwell on what you "should" have done. Don't buy into their game. Instead, replace the Guilt Gremlins with phrases such as:

"I get to..."

"I want to...",

"It would be helpful to...' and

"It fits with my values to..." And sidestep the guilt.

5. All or Nothing Gremlin

The All or Nothing Gremlin rears his ugly head when you are feeling angry or sad. When you're in a bad mood, you tend to view the world in absolutes – black or white, all or nothing, good or bad, possible or impossible. So if an event falls short of perfect, you may view it as a complete failure. For those of you on diets, it may occur when you have a bite of chocolate cake then think to yourself, "There I go again. I've completely screwed up my diet." And this thought often leads you to become more upset with yourself, in turn, eating more cake.

The initial thought "I've completely screwed up my diet" is simply not true. It's just a little mistake.

The world is never as simple as either/or, it is filled with various grays. The world does not lend itself to such simplistic dichotomies. Our world is too complex for these thoughts to be true.

Some examples of the All or Nothing Gremlin include:

"I'm the worst father on the planet" and

"None of the other kids like me" and

"If I do well on this presentation, then my boss will like me and give me a raise, but if I blow it then he won't like me and will fire me."

"I hate myself. I'm completely bad. There is no good in me"

"I'm completely stupid" and

"I am 100% worthless."

None of these thoughts are true. Yet, if you don't dispute and challenge them, you *risk making these negative thoughts true.*

The Negative Gremlin fills your head with false thoughts like, "I can't do anything right."

All or Nothing Gremlins are very, very rarely right. Ninety-nine percent of the time these thoughts are outright lies. Typically, these thoughts are fueled by sadness or anger. When you notice an All or Nothing Gremlin, take a step back and look at how you're feeling. If you are feeling angry, sad, or ashamed, it's a good bet your thoughts are messing with you.

When you become aware of such a Gremlin, challenge it. Is it based on reality? Is it true? Is it rational? When you challenge such thoughts, you remove its power over you freeing you to live *up* to your. potential.

6. The Negative Gremlin

This is similar to the All or Nothing Gremlin yet the Negative Gremlin focuses entirely on the negative and ignores the positive. Again, this Gremlin is deeply intertwined with how you are feeling. Negative feelings will greatly enhance the power of this Gremlin. When you are sad or mad, it becomes difficult to see that there are potentially positive outcomes in current situations. It becomes difficult to see that there are positive qualities in people whom you are angry with or whom you dislike.

The Negative Gremlin focuses completely on the negative and ignores anything positive. It's similar to filtering out all of the light and seeing only the dark. He insists that anything positive doesn't count. When this Gremlin strikes, positive remarks from others are rejected, positive experiences are discounted, and positive attitudes are put down. The problem with this Gremlin is that he sucks all the joy out of life. The Negative Gremlin, by focusing only on the negative, makes you feel inadequate and unworthy.

For example, Sam goes to a job interview. He's nervous. He's trying to present himself in the best possible light. Sam's not sure if the interviewer likes him or not. During the interview, the interviewer brings up his lack of experience for the job. At the end of the interview, the interviewer tells him, "So far you are the best candidate we've seen."

Sam focuses on the criticism and misses the positive feedback at the end. Shortly, he convinces himself that there is no way that he will get the job. He thinks, "They obviously didn't like me. I don't have enough experience. Why did I even bother going to that interview? I never had a chance."

Another Negative Gremlin for Sam might be, "I don't have anything to offer this company. They would be foolish to hire me. I'm sure there are many others who are far more qualified than me."

Sam came to these conclusions prematurely, *and* he ignored the interviewer's positive statement at the end of the interview.

The Negative Gremlin is deeply intertwined with how you are feeling. Negative feelings will greatly enhance the power of this Gremlin. When you are sad or angry, it becomes difficult to see that there may be positive outcomes in the situation.

Challenge your negative thoughts and feelings. Don't blindly accept them.

It is critical for your overall health and satisfaction with life to cultivate an attitude of optimism rather than pessimism. Research has shown that, with all other things being equal, optimists live, on average, seven and a half years longer than pessimists. Of course, to a pessimist, this may be a good thing. Many pessimists may be looking to get out of this life more quickly. After all, what use is a gift if you cannot see the beauty in it? I know. I've been there! Later in this book, I will cover ways in which you can foster an attitude of optimism.

7. The Overly Emotional Gremlin

The Overly Emotional Gremlin appears when you believe your negative feelings without questioning them. Feelings can lie to you as well. Many of us believe our feelings as truth without taking a closer look at them. For instance, I used to struggle with social anxiety which means that people made me nervous, especially large groups. When my social anxiety was prevalent, my feelings would tell me to run away from cocktail parties, business networking events, speaking engagements and fundraising events. My feeling of anxiety was telling me that these events were life-threatening and prepared me to fight or flee. Had I believed these feelings without questioning them, I would have fled. I wouldn't be writing this book. If I listened to my misleading feelings of fear, I'd be living alone in the wilderness.

"I am such an idiot!"

These Overly Emotional Gremlins can be identified because they usually begin with phrases such as "I feel …" Examples of such Gremlins include thoughts such as "I feel like I'm worthless," "I feel afraid," "I feel like nobody likes me," and "I feel like a failure." Any time you have a strong negative feeling, challenge it as soon as you become aware of it. Is there any evidence to support the feeling? Or is it just an irrational feeling? Are your feelings based on past events that no longer apply to the current situation? Occasionally, negative feelings are there to serve as a protection from real dangers. However, in our current world, our emotions are more likely to react to perceived dangers than real dangers. Your job is to pay attention to them, so you become skilled enough to tell the difference.

8. The Labeling Gremlin

The philosopher, Ludwig Wittgenstein, said, "When you label me, you negate me." Anytime you put a label on someone or something (including yourself), you reduce it to an oversimplified cartoon of its real self. By labeling someone a democrat, republican, old, young, gothic, rocker, businessman, prophet, artist, introverted, extroverted, sane, insane, smart, or dumb, you ignore and denigrate important parts that make up the whole of that individual. This is especially true of negative labels such as spoiled brat, idiot, dope, whiner, etc.

The Labeling Gremlin is not only hurtful; he has a way of becoming reality. When you call yourself an idiot, you run the risk of it becoming a self-fulfilling prophecy. Your expectations of yourself go a long way in defining who you are and how your life plays out. When you call someone else a dope, you unjustly lump them in with everyone else whom you consider a dope. This causes you to miss other positive parts of their being, such as good social skills, emotional awareness, or a loving heart. This also makes it more difficult to deal with them in a fair and productive manner. When you expect the worst of others, you will get it. When you expect the best, you will get the best.

9. The Blaming Gremlin

Many lives have been destroyed by the negative power of the Blaming Gremlin.

There are two ways for the Blaming Gremlin to operate. First, he convinces you that you are to blame for things that are out of your control. Second, he convinces you that others are to blame for things you can control.

Sometimes we hold ourselves too accountable. So you want to beware of holding yourself personally accountable for the outcome of any given event or situation. Oftentimes, the outcome hinges on far more than you and your possible actions. For instance, when your child struggles in school, you frequently blame your self, calling yourself a "bad parent" rather than trying to figure out the real cause of the problem.

And sometimes you may do the exact opposite and blame other people for your problems. When you do this, you overlook how you may be making the problem worse. For example, a father thinks, "I have a lousy relationship with my son because he never calls me. He's totally unresponsive." But has the father ever picked up the phone?

Those individuals that excel at screwing up their own lives are expert at blaming other people for their troubles. Nothing is their fault. When something goes badly in their life, education or work, they can always find another person or external event on which to lay the blame. They don't take ownership of their own problems and shortcomings.

Some examples of the Blaming Gremlin include phrases such as "That wouldn't have happened if you had…" and "It's not my fault that…" and "Why didn't you…" and so on. The basic (and faulty) argument is that "If you had just done something differently, I wouldn't be in this mess. This mess is your entire fault and I have no responsibility for it."

When you assign blame to others, you effectively render yourself powerless. You have just taken your power to effect change and given it to someone else. This is a big mistake.

Take personal responsibility for all your own mistakes, screw-ups and difficulties. You must cultivate an attitude of honest self-exploration. Mistakes are okay. They're natural. That's how you learn. All screw-ups are merely learning opportunities. On the other hand, when you have a success or triumph, give the credit to your hard work, ability or your higher power. In this manner, we are reminded to stay humble, continue to work

Blaming is a way to slough off personal responsibility. Yet, blaming gives your power to the one you blame.

on our development and growth, and share the credit for successful outcomes.

Don't let your life fall victim to the Blaming Gremlin.

10. The Perfectionistic Gremlin

The Perfectionistic Gremlin focuses on the 5% you got wrong when you scored 95% correct on a test. This Gremlin is never happy no matter how well you do. One mistake leads this Gremlin to conclude that you will never get it right. The Perfectionistic Gremlin sounds like:

"Why couldn't I get every question right? I am such an idiot!"

"We lost the game because of me. I stink!"

The Perfectionistic Gremlin also holds other people to the same unrealistic expectations. These are expectations that can never be met. Life isn't fair and perfection rarely shows up in this lifetime. This Gremlin will ensure that you are constantly unhappy and disappointed. The Perfectionist Gremlin also is highly related to eating disorders such as anorexia and bulimia.

Here are the ten types of Gremlin thinking presented in summary for you below.

The Perfectionistic Gremlin
is only happy when you are
perfect. The problem is that life
is rarely perfect!

Table 1.

Types of Gremlin Thinking

Gremlin Thought	Gremlin Type	How to Challenge the Gremlin
1. "I'm the worst at sports."	All or Nothing Gremlin	"This is not a rational thought. I'm not the worst. I just need more practice. Then, I'll improve."
2. "She is always mad at me."	Always or Never Gremlin	Watch for words like "always," "never," "no one," "everyone," "every time," and "everything."
3. "Others will just laugh at me and I'll look stupid."	Fortune Telling Gremlin	Try looking at worst case scenario or predicting the worst possible outcome. Is it all that bad? Replace negative thought with a positive image in your head ("They might like what I have to say."). Learn deep breathing techniques (e.g., diaphragmatic breathing).
4. "I know she doesn't like me."	Mind Reading Gremlin	Remind yourself you can't know another's thoughts. Reframe the situation more positively. "She might like me. Maybe she is having a bad day."
5. "I'm worthless."	Labeling Gremlin	I may do some dumb things, but I'm not worthless. Similar to 'All or nothing' thinking.
6. "It's all the fault of my boss."	Blaming Gremlin	What part did I play in creating the problem and how can we best solve it?
7. "I should do better in school."	Guilt –based Gremlin	Watch out for the words "should," "ought," and "have to." Reframe thought as "I want to…," "It would be helpful to…", or "It's in my best interests to…"

Gremlin Thought	Gremlin Type	How to Challenge the Gremlin
8. "I don't have a chance of making the soccer team."	The Negative Gremlin	Reassess situation when you are not in a bad mood. Look at evidence to confirm or deny your thoughts.
9. "I am such an idiot. How could I miss one of the extra credit problems on my math test?"	The Perfectionistic Gremlin	Practice forgiveness of yourself as well as others. Overcompensate by trying to make errors so you can eventually find a comfortable spot somewhere in the middle between perfect and error laden.
10. "I feel like a total failure when my team doesn't meet its sales goals."	The Overly Emotional Gremlin	Any time you have a strong negative feeling, challenge it as soon as you become aware of it. Is there any evidence to support the feeling? Or is it just an irrational feeling? Revisit the situation when you're in a better mood.

How Do You Tame Your Gremlins?

It is imperative that you become aware of your Gremlins and challenge them every time a Gremlin rears it's ugly, lying head. When you find a Gremlin, you can exterminate it by taking the following steps:

1. Realize that your thoughts are real. Thoughts can lead to real physiological reactions.
2. Become aware of how the Gremlin affects your body.
3. Become familiar with how your body reacts when you replace the Gremlin with a positive or happy thought.
4. Understand that your body reacts to every thought you have.
5. Think of Gremlins as an unwanted and undesirable infestation of your body.
6. Remind yourself that the Gremlin often lies to you.
7. Challenge the Gremlin. Question him. Talk back to him.
8. Imagine exterminating the Gremlin by sweeping him out of your head, stamping him Cancelled, squashing him with a shoe or flyswatter, or dropping him in the garbage can. Use your imagination!

Imagine you have a ninja in your mind, whose sole purpose is to eradicate Gremlins.

> *"We do not believe in ourselves until someone reveals that deep inside us something is valuable, worth listening to, worthy of our trust, sacred to our touch. Once we believe in ourselves we can risk curiosity, wonder, spontaneous delight or any experience that reveals the human spirit."*
>
> -- e. e. cummings

It is <u>critical</u> to question *every* thought that goes through your head. You must weed out the positive thoughts from the negative ones. Negative thoughts drain us of valuable mental energy. Listen to your positive and supportive thoughts. Actively challenge any negative or self-defeating thoughts. For example, if you have a critical thought such as, "I'll never get this right." Counter that thought with, "No, that's not true. I am smart. I am worthy. I will get this right." If you never challenge your negative thoughts and simply "believe them," then Gremlins will insidiously infiltrate your entire brain and eventually ruin your life. Instead, visualize a can of Gremlin spray to eliminate your negative thoughts, or Gremlin Police to come in, round up all your Gremlins and lock them up. This way you can snuff out the Gremlins who drain your mental energy.

Other Tips to Exterminate Your Gremlins

What objective data can you find to challenge your Gremlin? Look at the facts.

- Look at the available evidence. Does the evidence support or contradict your thoughts?
- See if you are applying a double standard which is different for yourself than for other people,
- Think of the situation or person in terms of grays (a scale of 1 to 100 where 1 is black and 100 is white with many shades of gray in between) rather than black and white,
- Take a survey of those around against which to gauge the thought. Ask how frequently

they think about such things and how important they are to them.

- Write out your worst case scenario, assuming the Gremlin thought is true. Could you live with this?

There are **numerous** ways to destroy these Gremlins. You are limited only by your imagination. The goal is to turn the negative thought into a positive thought. When you finally put a Gremlin to rest, you will experience a huge difference in the way you feel in your stomach. If you get stuck, keep trying different approaches until you get the right one.

Once you become more aware of your thoughts, you can choose to think good thoughts and feel peaceful or you can choose to think negative thoughts and feel angry, sad and ashamed. Train your mind to think positively. Learn how to change your thoughts and optimize your brain. Change your thoughts and renew your mental energy.

Watch your thoughts. Be on the look out for Gremlins. When you notice a Gremlin, question him, challenge him and talk back to him. When you challenge your Gremlins, you take away their power. Master your thoughts and feelings and you master your life.

> "Everything can be taken from a man or a woman but one thing: the last of human freedoms — to choose one's attitude in any given set of circumstances, to choose one's own way."
> Victor Frankl, Man's Search For Meaning

The Snowball of Thought

A brilliant analogy from Richard Carlson is to compare your thoughts to a tiny snowball. At first, the snowball is the size of your fist, something you could easily pick up and control. Now picture the snowball rolling down a large snow-covered mountain. As the snowball rolls down the hill, it picks up speed and grows exponentially. A short way down the hill, the snowball has already increased in size to the point

Your negative thoughts can run away with you, spiraling into a mammoth out-of-control snowball

where you can no longer handle it by yourself. Given the right conditions, the snowball can grow to mammoth size and could cause damage to yourself or other people.

The snowball is exactly the same as our thoughts. Each thought starts out tiny and manageable. However, if you are not paying attention, the thought spirals out of control and quickly creates unwanted effects.

The most important thing in controlling negative thoughts is confronting them. Don't simply accept them as truth. Tackle them. Check them out to make sure they are founded on fact, not fiction, and not feeling.

Decreasing Pain by Increasing Positive Expectations

You have a remarkable ability to reduce the intensity of pain that you experience. Think of the brain as having its own natural pharmacy. The human brain is capable of creating over 3000 chemicals. When the brain has a thought or feeling, the body responds by producing the necessary chemicals which are involved in many different types of physiological responses. One of the most fascinating is that our mind can learn to produce its own internal, natural painkillers – a group of small protein compounds (or neuropeptides) called endorphins and enkephalins. This response has been shown repeatedly in an effect that has been misunderstood by modern medicine for years, called the placebo effect. The placebo effect is the expectation of a pleasant effect, such as relief from pain, from something like a sugar pill that has no real medical benefits. This *positive expectation* actually causes the patient to experience less pain. The placebo effect occurs when the mind is convinced it will not feel pain so the nervous system produces endorphins and enkephalins.

> *"Whether you think you can or think you can't, you are right."*
> *Henry Ford*

So again, we have a situation where our thoughts and feelings come before our body's physical reaction. If you have an excited thought, then a molecule such as adrenaline arises and stimulates certain parts of the body. If you have a relaxing thought, a calm thought, then a 'calm' molecule is created that produces a restful effect on the body.

Amazingly, these molecules form an information network throughout your body. Due to this information network, any molecule in your body can communicate with any other molecule regardless of their distance from one another. We used to think that the cells had to be next to one another or have a physical means of communication. What we are finding is that our cells can 'talk' to one another *wherever* they are in our body.

Ways to Increase Positive Thinking and Realistic Optimism

Now that we've gone over what NOT to do, let's take a look at what you *can* do to foster positive thinking and restore your mental energy. The latest psychological research clearly demonstrates that the way in which your brain functions affects everything in your life – from your personal relationships, to your professional success, to your relationship with a higher power. By identifying and overcoming disorders such as anxiety and depression, you vastly increase the probability of having a positive personal relationship with your higher power.

The brain represents one of the last frontiers to be explored by human kind. There are many things you can do and we're just beginning to scratch the surface of the power of the mind. With that in mind, here are some of the more valuable ways to increase your positive mental energy:

- Coaching
- Change your negative habits
- Cultivate optimism
- Seek out the good in others
- Rewrite old tapes with new ones
- Realize that you are the good worth fighting for
- Think about thinking
- Stay focused in the present moment
- Learn to laugh and smile
- Blessings exercise
- Gratitude visit
- One door closes, another opens exercise

Coaching

Coaching is a means to assist individuals in identifying their core values and using those values to set long-term goals. Each long-term goal is broken up into smaller, achievable tasks. In this manner, I can assure the eventual success of my clients by continuing to break down larger, more imposing challenges into smaller and smaller acts. Coaching is a major asset for reprogramming the mental tapes, or thoughts, that run through your head. Oftentimes, these thoughts are so quick you aren't even consciously aware of them. Most times, these thoughts are negative and cause a negative reaction in our body. Coaching helps you to reprogram your old tapes so you can feed your brain healthy messages. It also provides you with a level of gentle accountability to ensure that you stick to your plan.

Change Your Negative Habits

Did you know that by changing your brain, you can change your life? You can. The brain relies on pathways between brain cells (neurons) to communicate messages from one area to another. You can create new pathways in your brain. You are capable of learning new ways of doing and being. To do so, you only need to do three things:

1. Become aware of your bad habit
2. Substitute a new and improved habit for the old one
3. Rehearse the new habit until it becomes automatic

When you learn new skills and attitudes, new pathways are created in your brain. The most efficient way to create these new pathways is by practicing the new task. The more you practice, the deeper engrained the pathway becomes in your brain.

The downside is that the more you continue to do the same old negative thoughts and behaviors, the more deeply engrained they become as well. However, you can change this at any moment by merely being aware of those thoughts you want to change and then consciously and intentionally substituting in a more positive thought.

Research has shown that our brain has the capability to create new pathways for as long as you live. This is exciting news because we used to believe the brain was incapable of growth and change after early adulthood. We now know that the brain continues to grow and adapt every day of our lives. Your brain is just like a muscle that needs exercise if you want to keep it in shape. And, believe me; you definitely want to keep your brain in shape!

Blazing a New Trail in Your Brain

Make your new phrase, "Retrain your brain."

At first, it seems difficult to learn a new skill or attitude. When you begin learning a new skill, the baby pathway between brain cells is like a hiking path in your brain. It's made of dirt and has pebbles and rocks on it. It is not very well-traveled so messages have a more difficult time "walking" from one place to another. The more you try out the new skill, the stronger the pathway becomes. After some practice, the pathway grows from a hiking trail into a two-lane highway. Now the messages move quickly and easily between the brain cells. Over time, the new skill becomes automatic and the two-lane highway solidifies into a super highway where the messengers of the brain rocket back and forth. The more you practice a new behavior, the more automatic and easier it becomes.

Just as physical skills such as running, jumping and playing sports become automatic through repetition, so too do thoughts, emotions and attitudes. As you repeat positive thoughts, your underlying pathways in the brain become stronger. Eventually, these paths become hardwired into your brain's circuitry.

Revisit Your Essential Core Beliefs

Your core beliefs, your stealthy, silent thoughts, matter tremendously. Take a close look at your core beliefs because they fuel your thinking. If your core beliefs are negative (e.g., "I always get the short end of the stick."), then your thinking will be negative. Negative thoughts lead to destructive emotions. So take a close look at your core beliefs, those things that you believe deep down in the core of your being.

While not scientifically proven, there seems to be a triad of negative beliefs which are at the root of all other destructive beliefs. These three beliefs stem from a confusion that arises when you mistake who you *are* with what you *do*. You are not what you do. You are not merely what you believe. You are not only what you feel. Those are aspects, facets, of you, but they are not the essence of you. You are far more than mere actions, beliefs, or feelings.

Many people make the serious error of rating how well they achieve followed by rating themselves as a good or bad person. Most folks judge their worth based on their achievements, their successes, and their failures. It's a ubiquitous error in judgment; everyone makes it unless taught otherwise. Logically, it seems to make sense. I, the individual, kick the ball well or poorly. The ball doesn't kick itself. So I 'logically' judge my kicking ability as good or bad. Then, I 'illogically' rate myself as a bad kicker, a bad athlete, or even a bad person. It's a mistake of overgeneralization. Most people overgeneralize from doing a bad act to being a bad person. That's a fallacy. It's wrong. Learn to separate your worth as an individual from your individual actions.

For example, I'm working with my nine year old son on the concept that he is far more than his ability on the baseball diamond. Whether he hits the ball well or not, he is still a great person. A bad day at the ballpark does not make him a bad individual. A bad act does not a bad person make. In the same vein, a good act does not *make* you a good person.

In order to be a bad person, you would have to consistently and frequently perform bad acts such as breaking the rules, not cooperating, and hurting others. This is hard to do and highly improbable. So even if you are responsible for a bad act, say kicking the ball poorly, you cannot judge yourself as a bad person. It's impossible to *be* what you *do*. A bad person would *only* and *always* behave in a negative manner. And a good person would act in a positive manner towards everyone at all times. Neither of these two extremes is possible.

The Three Most Damaging Core Beliefs

The three most damaging core beliefs that you can hold are as follows:

1) Other people MUST treat me fairly or they are bad people.
2) I MUST do well or else I am a bad person.
3) My life conditions MUST be the way I WANT them to be or I can't deal with it and will NOT be happy.

Stop "shoulding" all over yourself and others.

There are many other irrational beliefs that you might hold, but these three seem to be at the bottom of nearly every one of them. Integral to each and every one of your irrational, negative beliefs are the words "must", "should", or "ought."

The goal is to become aware of your negative core beliefs. Once you are aware of them, you can consciously substitute positive core beliefs for old, ineffective, untrue beliefs. Certain core beliefs have been proven to lead to greater well-being. The core beliefs that have been proven to work well are as follows:

Core Beliefs That Work Towards Well-being

1. You are incredibly important and matter tremendously to the rest of us.
2. You are not alone. You are surrounded by others who care.
3. There is no failure, only delayed success.
4. Lessons are repeated until learned.
5. Learning never ends.
6. The present is a better place to live than the past or the future.
7. While it may be difficult at present, you *can* handle it. Difficulties are temporary.
8. What you do with your life is entirely up to you.
9. All the answers lie within you. You have but to listen.
10. Always look for the good in people and events. You find what you look for.
11. Life is a roller coaster ride. Enjoy the ride.
12. Energy is limitless. You can tap into it at anytime.

Optimism: The Happy Boy and the Sad Boy

Once there were two brothers. One brother was happy and positive about everything. The other brother was negative and upset about everything. One Christmas, the boys' parents got them very different gifts. The negative boy received a Playstation2, some games and a battery powered remote control car. The positive boy got a large pile of horse manure. When the father asked the negative boy if was happy with his presents, the boy responded, "No I am not. The PlayStation2 games are difficult to learn and frustrate me. The remote control car won't work because the batteries are dead. This is an awful Christmas."

So the father went to the positive son and asked him how his Christmas was. The boy was hip-deep in horse shit, covered from head to toe, frantically digging through the pile. Smiling, he replied, "This is the best Christmas ever, Dad, with all this horse shit around, there *has* to be a pony in here somewhere!"

Cultivate an Optimistic Attitude

While you don't truly want to be hip-deep in horse manure, you do want to cultivate an optimistic attitude. Research clearly shows that optimistic individuals stay healthier, are more satisfied with life, live 7 - 10 years longer, are more resilient to difficult situations, and are better at loving their spouse. Cultivating an optimistic outlook will set a pattern of expectancy of positive results. Expecting positive results, the power of your thinking brain, helps to create those expected results.

How you respond to challenges, the dirt that life throws on top of you, is a tremendous indicator of how well you will succeed in school, in sports and at work. People with an optimistic attitude see setbacks as *temporary* challenges, challenges that can be overcome with effort. That one belief provides the foundation for perseverance and resilience that fuel high achievers. Optimism is the one trait which distinguishes superior performers from mediocre ones across nearly all areas of life – business, sports, education and relationships. So you say you need more convincing?

How do you deal with challenges?

Okay, let's consider the options – pessimism vs. optimism. There doesn't really seem to be a contest. Pessimistic people feel worse, look for the negative in events and people, have more negative emotions and are generally unpleasant to be around. What's more, they're right! If you look for the negative in any situation or person, you will find it. Yet, a pessimist is never satisfied. No matter who they are, how much money they have, what they do, who they surround themselves with, and it will never be enough. For the pessimist, by their nature, will find fault with all of it. How can a pessimist ever be happy? They cannot enjoy their family because they are busy finding faults and judging. To the extent that you are pessimistic and seek out the negative, you will find it and you will lead a miserable and unhappy life. I know. I used to be one.

You *want* to believe that good things will happen. Expectations, both positive and negative, have a way of coming true. The greater the extent to which you can picture your success, the greater the possibility of it coming to fruition. The more clearly you can envision your expected outcome the better. So you want to picture all the details you can imagine. Imagine the sights, the sounds, the smell, how you will feel when it happens, and who will be there. Paul Kingsman, an Olympic medal winner in the 200 meter backstroke, said that before a race, he pictured his race from every possible angle, from every lane, under every possible condition. This helped him to win the bronze medal and become the first person ever from New Zealand to win an Olympic medal.

The Case for Realistic Optimism

On the other hand, the optimist focuses on the positive. The optimist chooses to look for the good in people and situations. Please note that I said "chooses" because this outlook is a personal choice and it is always open to revision.

Optimism has been shown to have many positive health benefits. An optimistic outlook charges your inner battery with positive emotional energy and thus nurtures your resiliency. It helps you to heal from physical or emotional trauma more quickly. It helps you to support those around you when they suffer a setback. Optimism allows you to think more creatively and broadens your available options in terms of thinking and acting. It draws more optimistic people to you. Basically, optimism provides you with hope, and hope leads to peace. Research studies show that realistic optimists:

- Live 8 – 10 years longer than pessimists.
- Are more satisfied with their lives.
- Have better immune system functioning.
- Suffer from less anxiety and depression.
- Are more resilient.
- Are sick half as often as pessimists.

At work, an optimistic outlook leads to stronger relationships, better performance, more job satisfaction, and fewer sick days. In the insurance industry, studies report that:

- Optimistic sales advisors outsell the pessimists by 38%.
- Extremely optimistic advisors outsell extreme pessimists by 88%.

- Extremely pessimistic advisors are three times more likely to quit than extreme optimists

In the Real Estate industry, optimistic agents outsell pessimists by 33%. In banking, top performing salespeople are 25% more optimistic than below average performers. Top performing customer service representatives (CSRs) are *50% more optimistic* than below average CSRs. It's all in the way you look at (or perceive) the world.

Realistic optimists explain the events around them in a certain way. In other words, realistic optimists have certain attributional styles. They attribute their successes to internal causes and their failures to causes outside themselves (external causes). When *optimists* fail at something, they think to themselves "this is temporary, it's only for this one event, and I'm not the cause of it." When *optimists* experience a success, they think "this is permanent, the skill needed to accomplish this success holds true for all life events, and I'm the reason it happened."

Obviously, not all people are optimists. In my experience, a small percentage of people are realistically optimistic. At the other end of the spectrum from optimism is pessimism. Pessimists make sense of their life in a radically different manner from the optimists.

Thus, when *pessimists* are buffeted by difficult and *negative* events they say to themselves "this is permanent, my inability that caused this negative event is true for all situations, and my inadequate abilities are the cause of it." When *pessimists* encounter a success, or a *positive* event, they tell themselves "this is temporary, this is only for this one event, and I did not cause it."

Three Critical Dimensions to Realistic Optimism

There are three critical dimensions to realistic optimism. These dimensions are

1) **External vs. Internal:** The belief as to whether the *cause* of an event lies within us or outside of us,
2) **Permanence:** The belief that the cause of an event is permanent or temporary, and
3) **Pervasiveness:** The belief that the cause of the event is universal or particular.

Now you know that optimists and pessimists differ in that they explain life events differently, let me give you some examples.

An *optimist* explains the cause of *positive* events as being permanent, applying to all situations and internal (e.g., I succeeded because I'm good), and the cause of *negative* events as being temporary, particular to the one situation and external (e.g., I failed because that assessment was only examining one part of my ability and it was too difficult).

Realistically Optimistic Beliefs for Positive Events

1) For a realistic optimist, the CAUSES for POSITIVE events are *PERMANENT*
"I always give my best and work hard."
"I succeed at work because I'm a talented person."
"I raised good children because I am a good parent."
"I was promoted at work because I am a good employee."

2) For an optimist, CAUSES for POSITIVE events are *UNIVERSAL*

"I was promoted because I work very hard at everything that I do."

"I'm intelligent and capable."

"I am an attractive person."

"I finished that project on a tight deadline because I'm an efficient person."

"I saved a person from drowning because I know how to manage my emotions in tense situations."

3) For an optimist, CAUSES for POSITIVE events are *INTERNAL*

"I cause good things to come my way because of my positive attitude."

"My ability at soccer led to that goal."

"My students learn a great deal in my classes because I'm an effective teacher."

"I had a wonderful time at the office party because I am witty and outgoing."

Realistically Optimistic Beliefs for Negative Events

1) For an optimist, CAUSES for NEGATIVE events are *TEMPORARY*

"This fight with my spouse is only temporary."

"This too will pass."

"I'm tired today." (Instead of "I'm always tired.")

"My diet hasn't worked because I've been eating out too much lately."

"She nags me when she's in a bad mood."

2) For an optimist, CAUSES for NEGATIVE events are *PARTICULAR*

"I got a D on my paper because Dr. Schinnerer grades unfairly."

"I was fired because I made a mistake."

"My boyfriend/girlfriend cheated on me because he/she has a problem."

"This only has to do with work."

3) For an optimist, CAUSES for NEGATIVE events are *EXTERNAL*

"I'm not the cause of this."

"You didn't try hard enough."

"Relationships are hard for me because I grew up in a dysfunctional home."

"I lost to a person who was a stronger candidate with more experience."

The pessimistic pattern of explanations for life events is almost the exact opposite of optimistic explanations. *Pessimists* understand the cause of *negative* events as being permanent, universal and internal (e.g., "I failed because I'm bad"), and the cause of *positive* events as being temporary, particular and external (e.g., I succeeded because that assessment was only looking at one small part of my ability and it was easy).

Pessimistic Beliefs for Positive Events

1) For a pessimist, CAUSES for POSITIVE events are *TEMPORARY*

"After our fight, I made up with my spouse because I forgave him/her this one time."

"I was lucky today."

"I succeeded at work because I try hard."

"I raised good children because I am occasionally a good parent."

"I got promoted because I was the best choice today."

2) For a pessimist, CAUSES for POSITIVE events are *SPECIFIC*

"I'm smart at word problems."

"I'm good at speaking to small groups of subordinates."

"I finished that project on a tight deadline because I'm worked hard for a few weeks."

"I was witty and engaging with him."

3) For a pessimist, CAUSES for POSITIVE events are *EXTERNAL*

"I got lucky."

"My teammate's ability at soccer led to that goal."

"My students learn a great deal in my classes because the material is so strong."

"I had a wonderful time at the office party because other people were friendly."

Pessimistic Beliefs for Negative Events

1) For a pessimist, the CAUSES for NEGATIVE events are *PERMA-NENT*

"I am a failure."

"Dieting never works for me."

"She is always on my back, nagging me."

2) For a pessimist, the CAUSES for NEGATIVE events are *UNIVERSAL*

"All of my professors grade me unfairly."

"I was fired because I'm not good at anything."

"My boyfriend/girlfriend cheated on me because all men/women are no-good scum."

3) For a pessimist, the CAUSES for NEGATIVE events are *INTERNAL*

"I didn't try hard enough."

Relationships are hard for me because I'm self-centered."

"I lost because I didn't speak clearly enough at the campaign rallies."

The more pessimistic you are, the more likely you are to get down and stay down when bad things happen in your life. Negative events hit pessimists with greater force than optimists and pessimists will suffer for a longer time after a tragedy than optimists. So it makes sense, given all the research, to strive towards realistic optimism. After all, you'll live longer, live better, be happier, and enjoy more success.

Thoughts that typically will worsen your emotional state include things like:

"This always happens to me." The use of the word "always" implies a permanent state which is not true.

"I screw up everything in my life." The error here is overgeneralizing from one specific incident to every part of life.

"I screwed this up because I'm an idiot." The error in this thought occurs when you blame yourself when bad things happen. You take it too personally.

When bad things happen, you can blame your self, or other people and circumstances. People who blame themselves for failure have low self-esteem. They view themselves as worthless, talentless, and unlovable. This is NOT TRUE! Don't buy into that Gremlin thinking. You are a worthy individual. You just have to believe it!

People who blame others and circumstances don't lose self-esteem when bad events hit them. On average, they like themselves better.

Personalization, blaming yourself for failure, controls ONLY how you feel about yourself. Pervasiveness and Permanence are more important dimensions – because they control what you DO: how long you remain feeling helpless and across how many situations.

Do You Always Want To Be Optimistic?

Is it wise to be optimistic *all the time*? Or are there times when it makes sense to look for worst-case scenarios?

Most of the time, you want to be optimistic. However, there are times when it pays to be cautious. For instance, you don't want to be foolishly optimistic when your friend, who has been drinking, asks you for his car keys so he can drive home. You don't want to be overly optimistic and fail to take toilet paper with you on a camping trip thinking that you'll be able to grind the tree bark into soft, fluffy tissue.

You want to be optimistic in situations where you are trying to achieve such as academics, work projects and sports. It pays to be optimistic when you want to improve how you feel, when you want to be happier. Optimism is a wiser choice when you are dealing with a chronic health issue. Finally, optimism is the way to go when you are looking to inspire others around you.

You do NOT want to be overly optimistic when the stakes are high. When you are facing a risky, uncertain proposition, it pays to be cautious. Don't be optimistic when you are speaking with other people whose future looks bleak, such as a dying patient in the final stages of cancer. And you don't want to be overly optimistic with regards to others' troubles. So if your friend comes over to complain about her cheating husband, *stay away* from optimistic statements, such as "This doesn't have anything to do with you. Sex is only a small part of your marriage."

The main question to ask when considering where and when to be optimistic is: what is the penalty for failure? If the penalty is steep, then you are best off not using optimism. However, if the penalty is negligible, then you are best off using optimism.

Now that you know when to be optimistic, let's turn to one of the *proven* ways in which you can become more realistically optimistic.

ABCDE Method for Becoming More Realistically Optimistic

Albert Ellis, one of the founders of cognitive-behavioral therapy, has shown that people can change their attributional style (the way people explain life events) from pessimistic to optimistic.[74] Ellis' method is known as the ABCDE Method where A stands for Adversity, B is for Beliefs, C is for Consequences, D is for Dispute Negative Thoughts, and E is for greater Energy that arises from Effective New Ways of Viewing the World.

To use the ABCDE method, simply record your reactions to life events, and modify those reactions to be more optimistic. When doing so, pay attention to the adversity you face, the thoughts that arise, the consequences of those thoughts, how to best dispute negative thoughts. Once you've done that, it becomes much easier to arrive at effective new philosophies or ways of thinking about the world. Let me break it down more succinctly.

First, identify the **adversity** that you are experiencing or have experienced. That is, what bad event has happened to you?

Second, identify the **beliefs** that you are using to explain that bad event. That is, what attributions or thoughts do you have about the event? These beliefs might be hard to identify sometimes, because often they occur automatically. We have learned to explain the world using these beliefs so well that the explanations are automatic.

Third, examine the **consequences** of having that belief. That is, what do you do as a result of the belief? Many times a pessimistic attributional (belief) style will result in quitting, or avoiding, or ending an activity, so as to escape the bad feelings that the individual has experienced from facing adversity.

Fourth, to change the beliefs that you are using to explain the adversities you face, Ellis suggests using **disputation,** which involves (i) examining whether there is any evidence for the beliefs, (ii) identifying what the alternative explanations (beliefs) there are, (iii) what the implications of the belief are (does the belief really justify the consequences?), and (iv) what is the usefulness of the belief (is it really serving some function for me, or am I better off thinking something else?).

Fifth, the E in ABCDE stands for Energy or Effective New Thoughts. Generally, the consequences of negative beliefs are negative things, which often involve withdrawal from the situation and decreased enthusiasm for the situation or activity. Thus, changing the beliefs often leads to an increase in **energy,** such that the person feels good about what they are doing and they are looking forward to where they are going to go from here. What's more, changing your irrational, negative beliefs will lead you to adopting **effective new ways of looking at the world.**

Optimism is not intended to be simplistic positive thinking. Optimism is about thinking non-negatively, rather than thinking positively. You don't want to be a slave to positive thinking (optimism) any more than you want to be a slave to negative thinking (pessimism). However, by using optimism selectively you can have a better quality of life.

Seek Out the Good in Others

Actively look for good traits and noble deeds in other people. Only use positive and supportive language. When you compliment other people, be specific about the behavior you are praising. For example, rather than saying "Nice work," you might say, "Hey, you did a fantastic job closing the sale with Microsoft!" Remind those around you of their unique talents on a daily basis.

My wife and I try to be consistently aware of our attitude towards one another within our family. When things get stressful, and the family gets overly tired, we tend to slip into patterns where we attribute negative intentions to others. Oftentimes, these negative intentions are way off base. When we recognize this going on, we will stop what we're doing and have a family meeting where we all agree to give one another the benefit of the doubt and assume the other person has positive intentions. This helps get our family back to operating in a more positive and cooperative space.

Become More Aware of Your Internal Tapes

Watch the internal conversations that take place in your head. Challenge every negative thought that you have. Let go of your negative judgments about others AS WELL as yourself. Judgments are troublesome. Judgments create negative emotions such as guilt and shame and tear down self-esteem. Judgments are unfair. You can never be aware of the circumstances that have led another person to a particular point in their life. So you are never in a position to judge their actions and decisions.

Write over your old internal tapes with new ones of your own choosing. For example, let us assume that your mom told you that you were "a spoiled little brat" when you were a child. Whenever that tape gets played in your head, challenge it. Tell yourself, "Nope. That is NOT true. I was merely a child." Then, you can rewrite it as "I'm a generous person with great integrity and compassion."

The Power of the Present Moment

Now I want to share a little bit about the power of staying in the moment, in focusing your total attention to the task at hand. The elite athletes in the world know of the power of the present moment. Shouldn't you? By staying focused in the present moment, top athletes can shut out 80,000 angry, screaming fans to make a clutch pass, to sink a three pointer, or hit over a grand slam with the game on the line. It's all about absolute, total focus. It's about letting go of the mistake you just made. It's about letting the future take care of itself. Because the only thing that you can truly control, I mean really, truly control, in this world is your behavior right now. You can't change the past and the future hasn't happened yet. So the best you can do is make darn sure you are well prepared to take advantage of the moment in front of you – the right NOW.

If you're like most, your focus can be all over the map. Focus can shift between the inner world of thoughts and feelings, and the outer world, often called reality. Focus can be directed at the past, present or future. Your focus can be hijacked by your emotions, thoughts and a general lack of training and awareness. It takes practice to focus completely in this moment. Once you accept this moment just as it is, without judgment, you will be at ease in the here and now. Once you are at ease in the here and now, you will be comfortable in your own skin. You'll be comfortable with yourself. If you're anything like me, it will feel like quite an accomplishment. It took me nearly 35 years to figure out how to be comfortable in my own skin. I can't tell you what a peaceful feeling it is.

> **Exercise to Feel the Feeling of Being Totally Present**

Here's a way to get the feeling of being 100% present in the moment. Toss a tennis ball up in the air and catch it. Being 100% present in the moment is the feeling you have when the ball is in the air. It's the absence of thought. It is a feeling of being totally in the present. You aren't thinking about anything else. No worries. No frustration. No anger. No sadness. No negative thoughts. You just are. Now, the idea is to take that same focus and maintain it throughout your day. The idea is simple. Doing it is hard.you read any further.

In 2003, a study demonstrated that training employees of a fast-paced, high stress biotech company to stay focused in the present moment significantly decreased their anxiety, improved their immune system, and improved their satisfaction with life.[75]

By staying in the present moment, you can reduce the number of incorrect assumptions, judgments and perceptions, thus making your life more peaceful, joyous and meaningful.

Thinking about Thinking

Here is a new way of thinking that might help you understand the present moment a little more fully. Make sure your seatbelt is securely fastened, because this next bit may cause your mind to melt.

Inside you there is a being that does the thinking. You are not this thinker. I know this because I know that you can watch the thinker think. You can think about your thoughts. As soon as you begin to watch the thinker, you become aware of a new level of consciousness. In psychology, this is known as meta-cognition, or thinking about thinking. We also are capable of meta-emotion, or thinking about feeling.

The gist of it is that you need to tune in to the voice or voices in your head as frequently as you can. Pay close attention to those voices that repeat themselves over and over again. We have many, many old tapes that have been playing repeatedly in our heads for years, perhaps since you were a little child. This is what I'm talking about when I say "watch the thinker." As you listen to the voice, just listen to it. Don't judge what is being said. Soon you will realize that there is the voice AND there is a sense of your own being, a sense of "I am".

Once you realize that this higher level of awareness exists, you have begun to let the air out of your involuntary, obsessive thinking. Once you realize this higher awareness, you will find it easier to stay in the present moment.

Remember that earlier I said that your thoughts can lie to you. With this realization comes freedom from believing in your thoughts. Now you can question them, talk back to them, and challenge them.

You can practice being in the moment by taking any routine activity such as making the bed, journaling, filing, watering the lawn, washing dishes and give it your complete and utter attention. The task is no longer a means to an end. The task is the end in and of itself. Pay complete attention to the movement of every muscle in your body, the way you are holding your head, your back, and your breathing. Notice what every one of your senses is telling you as you perform the task. Notice the smells, the sights, the sounds, the taste, and the way in which it feels

The more you breathe deeply throughout the day, the easier it is to stay firmly rooted in the moment. Staying focused in the moment requires calmness and serenity which is aided by deep breathing. Now, the more you can learn to remain in the moment, the less you are troubled by destructive emotions such as anger and irritability. The less destructive emotions, the more likely you are to stay healthy and think clearly.

Limit Your Activities

More is NOT necessarily better. Slow your pace down. Physically slow your walk down. Take time to enjoy the world and people around you. Don't get caught up in the trap of being overly impressed with how busy you are. Busy-ness is not an indicator of importance nor is it an indication of satisfaction of life.

Become Appropriately Assertive

Assertiveness exists on a continuum between the poles of docile and aggressive. Think of assertiveness as a matter of degree; it exists on a 1 through 10-point scale where 1 is meek, 5 is assertive, and 10 is overly aggressive. Assertiveness deals with the ability to resolve disagreement and anger before it spirals into a destructive war. It is the ability to express one's feelings, thoughts, and needs clearly and explicitly and to defend one's rights in a constructive manner. Assertiveness falls somewhere between aggressiveness, at one end of the spectrum, and passivity at the other end.

Don't get caught up
in the death roll of anger...

Aggressive individuals will initiate unprovoked, menacing attacks that involve a violation of the rights of others. Examples of aggressive acts include bullying and harassment. Aggressive individuals frequently allow their anger to overtake them, causing a sort of death roll of emotion. Just like the alligator, the emotional mind can create a death roll of emotion where you spiral down into rage, destroying relationships and creating shame and resentment.

At the other end of the scale are individuals who are passive, timid, afraid of conflict and easily intimidated. Ideally, you will strike a nice balance between these two extremes.

For most people, assertiveness varies according to the situation. For example, the hard-nosed, results-driven executive may be highly assertive at work, yet be quite meek when it comes to dealing with his wife and teenage daughter at home. So assertiveness is environment-specific. Usually, your degree of assertiveness is couched within a role that you play – father, mother, spouse, boss, peer subordinate, friend, child and so on.

The goal is to learn how to be appropriately assertive without being a mean-spirited bully.

Most of us are wimps; wimps who do NOT know how to say "No" and stick to it. You may be a ubiquitous wimp, which means that you are wimpy in every situation, with every person. Others are situation-specific wimps. These wimps can be a tyrant at work and a pushover at home, forceful with strangers yet completely spineless with friends. Wimpiness can vary according to the situation. These wimps feel more comfortable being assertive in some areas of their life than others. Please understand that I use the term "wimp" with respect and understanding for I am a recovering wimp also.

Being a wimp works well in the short run because you don't risk upsetting anyone. You just let others have their way and no one's knickers get in a knot. However, in the long run, as you let people walk over you, your resentment gradually builds and your anger gets buried deep inside you. As you try to sit on more and more anger, your emotional gas tank eventually overflows resulting in irritation, outbursts of rage and passive aggressive behavior. You get angry at the wrong people, people who don't deserve your wrath. These repressed emotions also lead to physical symptoms such as headaches, stomachaches, high blood pressure, stroke, and heart attacks. In short, wimpiness is BAD for you and destructive to your health and happiness. If you want a life of meaning and happiness, if you want to perform at your best in life, you **must** learn to be appropriately assertive!

So what can you do? How do you stop being a wimp? How do you become appropriately assertive?

There are two sides to the assertiveness coin – being under-assertive and being too assertive, or aggressive. Being too aggressive is generally a matter of emotional management. You can learn to dial down your aggressiveness to the level of appropriate assertiveness by focusing your awareness on becoming more accepting, patient and forgiving. These areas are covered in more detail in the chapters on dealing with negative emotions and fostering positive emotions.

The other side of the assertiveness coin is learning what you want, what you will tolerate, and what is unacceptable. Once you have these areas clearly identified, you need to work on mustering the courage to state your needs aloud to others.

In general, you want to learn to love change because you are going to make some changes to your life and the way in which you interact with other people. You need to change some of the ways in which you think and act. Here are the specifics…

Figure out how you want other people to treat you…

Do you want your wife to stop yelling at you?

Do you want more respect from your husband?

Do you want your boss to speak to you in a normal tone of voice?

Do you want your children to help pick up the house?

The first step is to figure out what you want. Look at what is making you angry or irritated throughout the day. Make a mental note or write down each thing that is bothering you.

Also, figure out what you'd like to change in each relationship in your life. Where are you being taken advantage of? What are you tolerating? What are you putting up with? The first step is to unearth the answers to these questions.

Next, ask for what you want. This step takes courage, yet it gets easier the more you do it. And it's really not as hard as you believe it is. You must learn to express yourself, the real you; what you truly want; how you truly feel, if you want to be treated with more respect. When you learn to state how you feel and what you want, your whole life will begin to change for the better.

When you are asking for what you want, be as specific as possible. Keep it as short as possible and hold that thought in your mind, that way you can hold onto it even in the midst of an emotional conversation.

When stating your needs, the most effective form of communication is the following:

"I feel…when you do … and I need you to do …"

…where you fill in the blanks with your feeling(s), the act of the other person (if necessary), and what you need as a result. For example, "I feel angry and hurt when you come home late. I need you to come home at the time we agreed upon." You can use words to state the way you feel, your intentions or what you don't like. When you don't speak up, it's hard for people to know what your needs are.

To stop being a wimp, act with courage. It may feel awkward at first. Every new behavior feels a little strange at first. Yet within a few weeks, your authentic communication of your thoughts, feelings and needs will fit like a glove and you'll be wondering why you hadn't done it sooner.

Practice Saying "No"

Many of us have gotten in a dangerous habit of saying "yes" to every-one around us. However, it's merely a bad habit which *can* be changed. If you have trouble with saying "No", if that is too uncomfortable, use the phrase, "I'll think about it" or "Give me some time to think it over." This is just a temporary stop-gap. Using the phrase "I'll think about it" will hold off the other party for a time, but it raises your anxiety because you are only delaying giving a final answer. So realize that the ultimate goal is to be able to say "No" with a clear conscience. You have a right to say "No" to any request that comes your way. You have an obligation to take care of yourself first and foremost.

Identify What Makes You Afraid

Many of us wimps have created massive fears over what will happen if we DO say "No". We get into catastrophic, all or nothing Gremlin think-ing.

These are all irrational fears that have been blown up to monstrous proportions. Odds are that none of these things will actually happen if they stand up and rightly assert themselves. Remember to challenge your fears, your negative Gremlin thinking. Don't let them go by without speaking back to them. Check them against reality. Check your thoughts out with other people. What do people you trust have to say about it?

When you are dead, and your soul is reviewing your life here on earth, what do you want to see? Do you want to see yourself as a coward and a wimp who never stood up to shout the truth? Or do you want to look back and see a hero, a courageous individual who learned to speak out?

Assertiveness is NOT the same as aggressiveness. You don't have to be rude or impolite to be assertive. You don't have to attack someone to let them know of your thoughts and your feelings. You have the right to stand up for your rights. You have the God-given right to say "No" and to take proper care of yourself. Each and every one of us has rights. And you have the right to stand up and ask for what you want and need.

The worst that can happen is that they say "No. You can't have that."

Let me put it a different way. When you are dead, and you are looking back at the entirety of your life, what will you say was your favorite thing about life? What were you passionate about? What made you come alive? What made your blood race?

No matter what your answer, **you** need to know what makes **your** life worth living. And THEN you have to stand up for it. Ask for it. Fight for it. Work towards it. Pay attention to it.

You have to know what you want before you can be assertive. If you don't know, you can't ask.

To be assertive, you must know where your boundaries are; know what you want and how you want to be treated, and then stick to them. The main idea here is that you are **responsible** *to* others and *for* yourself.

Smile

Encourage and build up your sense of humor. Be quick to laugh and smile. You are never more in the moment that when you laugh. When you're laughing from the gut, your worries dissolve. True laughter is marked by an *absence* of thought. Build up a library of funny movies, stand up comedians, and humorous books. At the Guide to Self website (www. GuideToSelf.com), there is a running list of hilarious movies, CDs, and television shows. Revisit them often.

It is *so* simple to smile and yet we almost never do it. Smiling reduces tension. Smiling fills you up with energy. It makes you think you are happy and boosts your immune system functioning. Smiles and laughter exercise the heart. Smiling actually improves the quality of your relationships because people like to be around those who laugh easily and those who make them laugh.

Humor is difficult to pin down. It's real, yet it always eludes definition. No one is more transparent than someone trying to use humor to confront painful emotions, and transparency is one of the goals for a meaningful and happy life.

By the way, the word 'silly' actually comes from the Old English word *selig* which means to be happy, peaceful and blessed. So act silly – you'll feel better.

Learn Open-mindedness

It's helpful to have an open-mind when trying to stay focused on the moment at hand. Open-minded people make fewer judgments. Judgments focus on how you think the world SHOULD be. These are unenforceable rules that lead to disappointment and frustration. So work on having a flexible, open-mind. Entertain possibilities. Flexible people adjust to change. They bend as necessary to positively cope with situations. In the years that I spent studying what makes people successful in the workplace, one of the main factors was an attitude of being open to change. And you can see why – our world is in constant flux. There is very little that remains constant and unchanging in this day and age. We have to adopt an attitude of open-mindedness or risk being left behind, desperately holding on to outdated "the world is flat" ways of thinking. We have an innate yearning to endlessly discover, grow, and develop. We want to, we need to, evolve into more than what we are right now. One of the ways we do that is by having an open mind and staying in the present.

Blessings Exercise

Every night, write down 3 things that went well for you that day, even if you have had an awful day. You can still find 3 things that went well. Write them down and then write WHY they went well. This is a very simple exercise that has been proven to replenish your mental and emotional energy on a long-term basis. There is evidence that regular use of this exercise produces real lasting changes in your mood and mental energy.

Variations on the Blessings Exercise: If you are short on self-confidence, if you feel worth-less, write down 3 things that YOU did well that day. This will boost your self-confidence.

Here is an exercise from Martin Seligman, professor of psychology at Harvard, which has been shown to have a positive impact on your mood. It's called the gratitude visit.

Gratitude Visit

A gratitude visit is an exercise where you think of someone in your past who had a huge impact on your life but whom you've never really had the chance to thank. This has been proven in studies to be a life-changing exercise. Simply think of someone who you never had the chance to properly thank who got you headed in the right direction or saved you from going in the wrong direction. Next, during the next week, you write a five-hundred word testimonial to them telling them how they were so important to you. And most people who do this exercise write a first draft, then a second draft and often feel like they can't get it quite right. That's okay. Just do the best you can. Whatever you come up with will ultimately be fine. When you're finished, call the person up and see if they are willing to meet for coffee. You don't have to say why you want to see them. When you see them, just read what you've written about them to them. And then happiness and appreciation and hugging follow. Then you can talk more about what an influence the person had on your life. Everyone feels renewed and refilled with positive thoughts and feelings.

Here is another exercise called Three Questions that will help you to create more positive emotions in your life.

Three Questions Exercise

This one is quick and simple. Every day ask yourself the following three questions and then answer them:

Where did I come from?

How is it going right now?

Where am I headed?

Let me explain so you will have an idea how to answer these questions.

1. Where did I come from?

This question is all about your attitudes and the way in which you understand your past. How you explain past experiences and relationships to yourself reveals your basic attitudes. And it is these attitudes that shape your reaction, good or bad, to *every* event that takes place in your life.

Unhappy people ask themselves "Where did I come from?" and see themselves as a victim. They see disaster, broken relationships, and weakness. Then they look for AND FIND evidence that supports their pessimism.

On the other hand, happy people ask themselves, "Where did I come from?" and see triumphs over challenges. They see the lessons they've learned. They see solutions, strengths, and gratitude. They look for and FIND things that support their optimism. The main lesson here is that we become what we think.

2. How is it going right now?

This question has to do with the degree to which you are comfortable in your own skin in the present moment. Your relationship with yourself is constantly changing. It changes minute to minute based on internal and external events. Happy individuals revisit their self-image consistently. They take responsibility for their mistakes and give credit for success to God. They know they are responsible for their own thoughts, feelings and actions. And when they begin to act inappropriately, they are able to self-correct their behavior so they return to the proper path.

Unhappy people tend to stay away from self-assessment because it is painful. However, self-reflection pumps up our spirit the same way exercise pumps up our body. Self-reflection strengthens our inner resources and our ability to mold our future.

One of the ways that you can do this is to write down three negative beliefs that you have about yourself. For instance, "I'll never amount to anything", "I'll never be able to provide for my family", "I'm a loser", "I'm stupid", "I'll never reach my normal weight", and so on. Second, challenge those beliefs. Simply accept the possibility that you may be wrong in your negative self-assessment. The way to challenge those beliefs is to write down 2 or three reasons that each of your negative beliefs may be wrong. If you have trouble with this, ask your loved ones for help and suggestions. Third, introduce any new evidence that contradicts your beliefs such as compliments, identifying your good traits, and things that are working for you. Fourth, reinterpret your past with grace and forgiveness. While reinterpreting your past, remember that every painful experience in life has some positive lesson buried within it. Your job is to find the meaning in the muck and the mire of your past. Look to uncover the lessons that you've learned as a result of past difficulties. Once you find meaning in them, they lose their emotional weight. Finally, change the way you talk to yourself. If you find you are insulting yourself, replace the names and putdowns with encouraging and supportive words. Treat yourself with the same love and compassion that you would treat a small child.

3. Where are you headed?

This question has to do with your values, strengths and motivations. The ability to accomplish something is strongest when our values, strengths and motivation are in synch. Happy individuals who have a sense of purpose in their lives have a clear vision that helps them to keep moving forward when things get difficult, because inevitably, things will get difficult. Happy people have a unique, personal definition of success that keeps them from staying down when they get down. This definition of success helps them to bounce back from difficult situations.

For instance my definition of success states that I am a man of God, husband to one, father of three, soon-to-be four, and a psychologist intent on bridging the gap between psychology and spirituality. Sometimes I fall short of that, but when I do, I know that motivation comes from within. Motivation is a combination of your physical, mental, emotional and spiritual energies. Strengthening your inner resources is just like strengthening your muscles. You need to stretch and strengthen your beliefs, your emotions, your thoughts and your actions.

Remind Yourself of the Good in the World

One of my reasons for writing this book is to remind you of the good that exists in our world. *You* are part of that good. You are good. It's essential that we continue struggling to spread the good, the joy, every moment of every day that you draw breath. If you do that, you will be fulfilling your purpose, your destiny, your life will have meaning, and you will be happy. At that point, you will live without regret, without worry of lies or exaggerations tripping you up, without fear of death even, because you will know, at the end of the day, that you have given *everything* you have, you've given it your *all*. When you live your life to its potential, when you act according to you dearest values, when you manage your emotions, steer your thoughts, and speak to God, then YOU become the good worth fighting for.

And that's what I'm trying to *inspire* you to do – you must *wake up* to life; *stop* waiting to die and *start* wanting to live. Don't settle for mediocrity and normalcy. Strive for greatness. Don't stop until you're living an exemplary life. Realize that YOU set the bar for others. Set it high on every level – physical, ethical, emotional, mental and spiritual. You ARE the example for others.

So how do you go about doing that? Odds are that you are already doing much of it if you're reading this book. The burning question is "Are you doing ALL of it? Are you pushing the envelope in each of the six areas? Do you know what your top values are? Are you in great physical shape? Can you manage your emotions? Do you know how to stay positive amidst trouble? How strong is your relationship to God? Are you surrounded by positive people? Realize that a weakness in any one of these areas can cause a whole life to collapse. Let me give you an example.

Ted is a deeply spiritual man who speaks daily to God through prayer. He is physically fit, running five miles daily. He knows what his top values are and lives according to them. Yet, he is weak in one area – managing his own emotions. When his children misbehave, his anger erupts. He yells at them, making his children believe they are bad people, undermining their self-confidence and causing fear and anxiety to take root in them. His children will grow up to resent and reject God because of the behavior of their father. Ted's wife fears his unpredictable moods – irritation, withdrawal, sadness, anger, and impatience fill most of his days. Due to his poor emotional control, Ted risks undermining his values which include treating others with respect and love. He risks an unbalanced spiritual life by setting a poor example for his loved ones, an example that is in direct contradiction of the behaviors modeled by Jesus. Ted's negative emotions also eat away at his physical health for we now know that anger and irritation are directly related to greater risk of stroke, heart attacks, low self-esteem, migraines, ulcers, substance abuse problems. Finally, Ted's difficulty with anger has been shown to lead to troubled relationships at work and with friends and family. It also will interfere with his financial situation because it's likely to lead to frequent job loss.

As it goes with the management of your emotions, so it goes with each of the other critical areas – physical health, relationship with God, mental health, awareness of values and supportive relationships. You cannot lead an exemplary life by excelling in only one or two of these. Focusing on one or two of these areas is not sufficient for an extraordinary life. Weakness in any one of these areas is enough to destroy a lifetime of hard work. Each of these areas interacts with and has an effect on every other area. They are interconnected. You can't simply ignore one area and hope it goes away. The chain is only as strong as the weakest link.

You have to focus on strengthening and becoming more aware of each of these areas to create your extraordinary life.

Remember, YOU are the good worth fighting for.

As Gandhi said, "You must be the change you wish to see in the world." If you want to create a better world, you have to begin with yourself. Only then can you truly help others.

For further information on coaching programs or keynote speaking engagements, contact Dr. John at Info@GuideToSelf.com or visit www.GuideToSelf.com. Have a wonderful life!

Live Happily Ever After,
Dr. John

Additional Resources

Bradberry, T. & Greaves, J. (2003). *The Emotional Intelligence Quickbook*. Talentsmart. San Diego.

Damasio, A. (1994). *Descartes' Error: Emotion, Reason and the Human Brain*. New York. Grosset/Putnam.

Gilbert, D. (2006). *Stumbling on Happiness*. Alfred A. Knopf. New York, NY.

Goleman, D. (1995). *Emotional intelligence: Why it can matter more than IQ*. Bantam, New York.

Levenson, R.W., Ekman, P., & Friesen, W.V. (1990). Voluntary facial action generates emotion-specific autonomous nervous system activity. *Psychophysiology*, 27.

Mayer, J.D. & Salovey, P. (1993). The Intelligence of Emotional Intelligence. *Intelligence*. 17(4), 433-442.

Mayer, J.D., DiPaolo, M.T. & Salovey, P. (1990). Perceiving affective content in ambiguous visual stimuli: A component of emotional intelligence. *Journal of Personality Assessment*, 54, 772-781.

Payne, W.L. (1985). A study of emotion: Developing emotional intelligence: Self integration, relating to fear, pain and desire. Unpublished doctoral thesis, The Union Inst., Cincinnati, OH.

Thorndike, E.L. (1920). Intelligence and its uses. *Harper's Magazine*, 140, 227-335.

Endnotes

[1] Haidt, J. *The Happiness Hypothesis.* 2006. Basic Books, Cambridge, MA.

[2] Ekman, P. *Emotions Revealed.* 2003. Henry Holt and Co. New York, NY.

[3] Seligman, M. *Authentic Happiness.* 2002. Simon & Schuster. New York, NY.

[4] The Dalai Lama & Cutler, H. *The Art of Happiness.* 1998. Riverhead Books. New York, NY.

[5] Loehr, J. & Schwartz, T. *The Power of Full Engagement.* 2003. Free Press. New York, NY.

[6] Buckingham, M. & Clifton, D. *Now, Discover Your Strengths.* 2001. Free Press. New York, NY.

[7] Amen, D. *Change Your Brain, Change Your Life.* 1998. Times Books. New York, NY.

[8] Roizen, M.F. & Oz, M.C. *You: The Owner's Manual.* Harper Resource. New York, NY.

[9] Haidt, J. *The Happiness Hypothesis.* 2006. Basic Books, Cambridge, MA.

[10] Fredrickson, B.F. & Losada, M.F. (2005). "Positive Affect and the Complex Dynamics of Human Flourishing." American Psychologist, October 2005, 60, 7, 678-686.

[11] Fredrickson, B.F. & Losada, M.F. (2005). "Positive Affect and the Complex Dynamics of Human Flourishing." *American Psychologist,* October 2005, 60, 7, 678-686.

[12] Fredrickson, B.F. (2001) "The Role of Positive Emotions in Positive Psychology: The Broaden-and-Build Theory of Positive Emotions" *American Psychologist,* March, 56, 3, 218-226.

[13] Ekman, P. 2003. *Emotions Revealed.* Henry Holt and Company, New York.

[14] Ekman, P. 2003. Ibid.

[15] Gross, J. & Levenson, R. W. (1997) "Hiding Feelings: The Acute Effects of Inhibiting Negative and Positive Emotion." *Journal of Abnormal Psychology*, 106, 1, 95-103.

[16] Raikkonen, K., Matthews, K.A., Flory, J.D., Owens, J.F., and Gump, B.B. (1999) "Effects of Optimism, Pessimism, and Trait Anxiety on Ambulatory Blood Pressure and Mood During Everyday Life." *Journal of Personality and Social Psychology*, 76, 1, 104-113.

[17] Fitzgerald, T. E., Tennen, H., Affleck, G., & Pransky, G. S. (1993). "The relative importance of dispositional optimism and control appraisals in quality of life after coronary artery bypass surgery." *Journal of Behavioral Medicine*, 16, 25-43.

[18] Larsen, R. J., & Kasimatis, M. (1991). "Day-to-day physical symptoms: Individual differences in the occurrence, duration, and emotional concomitants of minor daily illnesses." *Journal of Personality*, 59, 387-423.

[19] Raikkonen, K., Matthews, K. A., Flory, J. D., & Owens, J. F. (1999). "The effects of hostility on ambulatory blood pressure and mood during daily living in healthy adults." *Health Psychology*, 18, 44-62.

[20] Zautra, A., Smith, B., Affleck, G., and Tennen, H. (2001) "Examinations of chronic pain and affect relationships: Applications of a dynamic model of affect." *Journal of Consulting & Clinical Psychology.* 69(5), Oct, 786-795.

[21] Salovey, P., Detweiler, J.B., Steward, W.T., and Rothman, A.J. (2000) "Emotional States and Physical Health." American Psychologist, Jan 2000, 55, 1, 110-121.

[22] Suls, J., Bunde, J. (2005) "Anger, Anxiety, and Depression as Risk Factors for Cardiovascular Disease: The Problems and Implications of Overlapping Affective Dispositions" Psychological Bulletin, March 2005, 131, 2, 260-300.

[23] Ekman, P. (2003) *Emotions Revealed.* Henry Holt and Company, New York.

[24] Frederickson, B. & Branigan, C. "Positive Emotions." In T.J. Mayne and G. A. Bonnano (Eds.), *Emotion: Current issues and future directions.* New York: Guilford Press. (2001), 123-151.

[25] Fredrickson, B. "The role of positive emotions in positive psychology: The broaden-and-build theory of positive psychology." *American Psychologist.* March 2001, 56, 3, 218-226.

[26] Fredrickson, B. & Levenson, R.W. (1998). "Positive emotions speed recovery from the cardiovascular sequelae of negative emotions." *Cognition and Emotion*, 12, 191-200.

[27] Baumeister, R.F., Bratslavsky, E., Finkenauer, C. and Vohs, K.D. (2001) "Bad is Stronger than Good." *Review of General Psychology*, December 2001, 5, 4, 323-370.

[28] Lama, Dalai, Goleman, D., *Destructive Emotions: How can we overcome them?* 2003. New York: Bantam Books.

[29] Fredrickson, B. (2001). "The role of positive emotions in positive psychology: The broaden-and-build theory of positive emotions." *American Psychologist*, March, 56, 3, 218-226.

[30] Seligman, M.E. & Royzman, E. (2003). "Happiness: The three traditional theories." *Authentic Happiness Newsletter*. July 2003.

[31] Emmons, R. A., & McCullough, M. E. (2003). "Counting blessings versus burdens: An experimental investigation of gratitude and subjective well-being in daily life." *Journal of Personality and Social Psychology, 84,* 377-389.

[32] Watkins, P. C. (2004). "Gratitude and subjective well-being." In R. A. Emmons & M. E. McCullough (Eds.), *The Psychology of Gratitude* (pp. 167–192). New York: Oxford University Press.

[33] McCullough, M. E., Tsang, J., & Emmons, R.A. (2004). "Gratitude in Intermediate Affective Terrain Links of Grateful Moods to Individual Differences and Daily Emotional Experience." Journal of Personality and Social Psychology, February, 86, 2, 295-309.

[34] Peterson, C. & Seligman, M. Character Strengths and Virtues: A Handbook and Classification. 2004. Oxford University Press.

[35] Gable, S. L., Reis, H.T., Impett, E. A., & Asher, E.R. (2004). "What Do You Do When Things Go Right? The Intrapersonal and Interpersonal Benefits of Sharing Positive Events." *Journal of Personality and Social Psychology,* August 87, 2, 228-245.

[36] Reitman, J. (2005). "Surviving Fallujah." *Rolling Stone*, March 10, 2005.

[37] Brickman, P., Coates, D. & Janoff-Bullman, R. (1978). "Lottery winners and accident victims: Is happiness relative?" *Journal of Personality and Social Psychology*, 36, 917-927.

[38] Shapiro, S.L., Astin, J.A., Bishop, S.R., and Cordova, M. (2005) "Mindfulness-Based Stress Reduction for Health Care Professionals: Results From a Randomized Trial." *International Journal of Stress Management,* May 2005, 12, 2, 164-176.

[39] Kabat-Zinn, J., Wheeler, E., Light, T., & Cropley, T. G. (1998). "Influence of a mindfulness meditation-based stress reduction intervention on rates of skin clearing in patients with moderate to severe psoriasis undergoing phototherapy (UVB) and photochemotherapy (PUVA)." *Psychosomatic Medicine, 60,* 625-632.

[40] Davidson, R., et. al. "Alterations in brain and immune function produced by mindfulness meditation." Psychosomatic Medicine. In press.

[41] Davidson, R., et. al. Ibid.

[42] Seligman, Martin. *Learned Optimism.* 1998. New York. Pocket Books.

[43] Kabat-Zinn, J., Massion, A. O., Kristeller, J., Peterson, L. G., Fletcher, K. E., et al. (1992). "Effectiveness of a meditation based stress reduction program in the treatment of anxiety disorders." *American Journal of Psychiatry, 149,* 936-943.

[44] Miller, J. J., Fletcher, K., & Kabat-Zinn, J. (1995). "Three-year follow-up and clinical implications of a mindfulness meditation-based stress reduction intervention in the treatment of anxiety disorders." *General Hospital Psychiatry, 17,* 192-200.

[45] Haidt, J. *The Happiness Hypothesis: Finding Modern Truth in Ancient Wisdom.* 2006. New York. Basic Books.

[46] Beck, A.T., Rush, A.J., Shaw, B.F., and Emery, G. *Cognitive Therapy of Depression: A Treatment Manual.* New York. 1979.

[47] Fredrickson, B. (2001). "The role of positive emotions in positive psychology: The broaden-and-build theory of positive emotions." *American Psychologist,* March, 56, 3, 218-226.

[48] Butler, E.A., Egloff, B., Wilheim, F.H., Smith, N.C., Erickson, E.A., & Gross, J.J. (2003) "The social consequences of expressive suppression." *Emotion,* 3, 48-67.

[49] Salovey, P., Rothman, A.J., Detweiler, J.B., & Stewart, W.T. (2000). "Emotional states and physical health." *American Psychologist,* 55, 110-121.

[50] Csikszentmihalyi, M. *Finding Flow: The Psychology of Engagement with Everyday Life.* 1997. Basic Books.

[51] Goleman, D. *Emotional Intelligence.* 1995. New York: Bantam Books.

[52] Salovey, P. and Mayer, J. (1990). "Emotional Intelligence," *Imagination, Cognition, and Personality,* 9, pp. 185-211.

[53] Fredrickson, B. (2001). "The role of positive emotions in positive psychology: The broaden-and-build theory of positive emotions." *American Psychologist,* March, 56, 3, 218-226.

[54] Bonnano, G.A. (2004). "Loss, trauma, and human resilience: Have we underestimated the human capacity to thrive after extremely aversive events?" *American Psychologist*, January, 2004, 59, 1, 20-28.

[55] Damasio, A. *Descartes' Error: Emotion, Reason and the Human Brain.* 1994. New York. Grosset/Putnam.

[56] Childre, D. and Martin, H. *The HeartMath Solution*, 1999. HarperSan-Francisco.

[57] Childre, D, and Martin, H. *The HeartMath Solution*, 1999. HarperSan-Francisco,

[58] Hiemke, C. Circadian variations in antigen-specific proliferation of human T lymphocytes and correlations to cortisol production. *Psychoneuroendocrinology.* 1994: 20:335-342.

[59] Manolagas, S. Adrenal steroids and the development of osteoporosis in the oophorectomized women. *Lancet.* 1979;2:597.

[60] Marin, P. Cortisol secretion in relation to body fat distribution in obese pre-menopausal women. *Metabolism.* 1992;41:882-886.

[61] Sapolsky, R. *Stress, the Aging Brain, and the Mechanisms of Neuron Death.* 1992. Cambridge, MA: MIT Press.

[62] Luskin, F. *Forgive For Good.* 2005.

[63] Bonnano, G.A., Noll, J.G., Putnam, F.W., O'Neill, M., & Trickett, P. (2003). "Predicting the willingness to disclose childhood sexual abuse from measures of repressive coping and dissociative experiences." *Child Maltreatment*, 8, 1-17.

[64] Keltner, D., & Bonanno, G.A. (1997). "A study of laughter and dissociation: Distinct correlates of laughter and smiling during bereavement." *Journal of Personality and Social Psychology*, 73, 678-702.

[65] Shimanoff, S. B. (1985). "Rules governing the verbal expression of emotions between married couples." *Western Journal of Speech Communication*, 49, 147-165.

[66] Cappas, N.M., Adnres-Hyman, R., & Davidson, L. (2005). "What Psychotherapists Can Begin to Learn from Neuroscience: Seven Principles of a Brain-Based Psychotherapy." *Psychotherapy: Theory, Research, Practice, Training*, Fall 2005, 42, 3, 374-383.

[67] Melzack, R., & Wall, P.D. (2003) *Handbook of Pain Management.* New York: Elsevier Science.

[68] Gaudreau, P. & Blondin, J.P. (2004). "Differential Associations of Dispositional Optimism and Pessimism With Coping, Goal Attainment, and Emotional Adjustment During Sport Competition." International Journal of Stress Management. August 2004, 11, 3, 245-269.

[69] Sheldon, K. M., & Houser-Marko, L. (2001). Self-concordance, goal attainment, and the pursuit of happiness: Can there be an upward spiral? *Journal of Personality and Social Psychology, 80,* 152-165.

[70] Puskar, K. R., Sereika, S. M., Lamb, J., Tusaie-Mumford, K., & McGuinness, T. (1999). Optimism and its relationship to depression, coping, anger, and life events in rural adolescents. *Issues in Mental Health Nursing, 20,* 115-130.

[71] Chang, E. C., Sanna, L. J., & Yang, K.-M. (2003). Optimism, pessimism, affectivity, and psychological adjustment in U.S. and Korea: A test of a mediation model. *Personality and Individual Differences, 34,* 1195-1208.

[72] Amen, D. *Change Your Brain, Change Your Life.* 1999. Three Rivers Press. New York, NY.

[73] Gilbert, D. *Stumbling on Happiness.* 2006. Alfred A. Knopf. New York, NY.

[74] Ellis, A. *Rational Emotive Behavioral Therapy.* 2004. Prometheus Books. Amerst, NY.

75 Davidson, R., et. al. "Alterations in brain and immune function produced by mindfulness meditation." *Psychosomatic Medicine.* In press.

About the Author

Dr. John Schinnerer has a Ph.D. in psychology from the University of California at Berkeley. He has 12 years experience in research and practice. Dr. Schinnerer has been on the path of self-knowledge and discovery since the age of 17. His passion is the point of intersection between spirituality, psychology, philosophy and biology. Dr. Schinnerer has stressed the need for greater awareness in health, psychology and the mind-body connection. He openly acknowledges the need for clear values and a strong faith as the core of a happy and meaningful life, putting him on the cutting edge of mental health professionals.

Dr. Schinnerer founded Infinet Assessment, a psychological testing company in 1997. The new methodology he developed looks at emotional IQ, traditional IQ, ethics, personality traits, and knowledge. This methodology was shown to reduce turnover at UPS by 34%. He is an expert in the evaluation of those competencies necessary for successful job performance. His areas of expertise include uncovering traits necessary for success in the workplace and life, psychological assessment, leadership development, business communication, emotional intelligence, and corporate culture.

Dr. Schinnerer has written articles for Workspan, HR.com, HRnext, and several papers. Dr. Schinnerer also reviews articles for WorldAtWork. He is currently authoring a follow-up book which is a business parable to teach individuals, particularly business people, the importance of, and how to, emotional self-awareness and self-control (or how to control your emotions without suppressing them). This is one of a number of essential life skill parables to be written. It is the first in a series of books using the fictional story format (the most effective means of reaching others) to teach each of the emotional intelligence competencies

Currently, Dr. Schinnerer is the President of Guide To Self, a company dedicated to improving our mastery of our body, mind, spirit and relationships. Guide To Self revolves around the daily radio program, "Guide To Self Radio", which airs Monday through Friday at 5 pm on 1640 AM in the San Francisco Bay Area. The show promotes best practices for mental, physical and spiritual well-being through a compelling blend of story-telling and facts backed up by scientific research. This combination of story and fact is purposely designed to tap into both sides of the minds of the listeners – the emotional mind and the rational mind.

Dr. Schinnerer has found in his counseling that a belief in God is essential for a contented and meaningful existence. The particular path to God isn't as important as the presence of a daily, personal relationship with one's own Higher Power. Thus, he is in a unique position to bridge the gap between science and spirituality. Most importantly, he has a sense of humor. The successful changes he has made in his own life and practice prove that he is a man of vision and deeds whose attitudes arise from the truths of living moment-to-moment with his wife and their four children.